THE LAW COMMISSION

CONSULTATION PAPER No. 125
STRUCTURED SETTLEMENTS AND INTERIM AND PROVISIONAL DAMAGES

TABLE OF CONTENTS

LIBRARY
DEPARTMENT OF SOCIAL SECURITY
ROOM 07/15 ADELPHI
1 - 11 JOHN ADAM STREET
LONDON   WC2N 6HT

171497

ADI

SFP
1992
F

346.0323 STR

The Law Commission
Consultation Paper No. 125

Structured Settlements and Interim and Provisional Damages :

A Consultation Paper

WITHDRAWN FROM STOCK

LIBRARY
DEPARTMENT OF SOCIAL SECURITY
ROOM 07/15 ADELPHI
1 JOHN ADAM STREET,
LONDON   WC2N 6HT

LONDON: HMSO

© *Crown copyright 1992*
Applications for reproduction should be made to HMSO
First published 1992

ISBN 0 11 730208 2

APPENDIX C

APPENDIX D

PART I

INTRODUCTION

The Scope of the Paper

1.1   This paper is the first consultation paper arising from the Law Commission's current examination of the principles governing and the effectiveness of the present remedy of damages for monetary and non-monetary loss, with particular regard to personal injury litigation.[1] The Commission returns to the topic after a gap of nineteen years[2] during which much has happened. This paper addresses aspects of the question of whether the damages remedy is effective, and how it can be made more effective. It canvasses the deficiencies of lump sum damages, and considers whether the development of voluntary structured settlements,[3] and the existing provisions for interim and provisional payments, usefully correct such deficiencies.

1.2   In the case of structured settlements, developments in the United Kingdom have been influenced by their tax treatment. It is accepted that in certain circumstances payments to a plaintiff arising from an annuity arranged by a defendant will be capital and therefore not taxable in the hands of the recipient. We shall consider whether there is scope for rationalisation of the tax arrangements to eliminate anomalies. We shall also consider whether there should be a more fundamental reform of the voluntary system of structured settlements by the creation of a power in the court to require that an award be structured, and of the tax regime. The paper takes account of the experience in the United States and Canada where structured settlements were pioneered.

1.3   The arrangement of the paper is as follows. Part II considers lump sum awards and in particular the approaches to the calculation of future loss. Although this latter question has been the subject of much previous consideration, the appearance of Index-Linked Government Securities, and the increasing use of structured settlements, gives it a new importance. This is because, while lump sum awards are based on the multiplier/multiplicand method used by the courts, the annuities which make up a structured settlement are based on an actuarial assessment of future loss. Part III considers structured settlements, Part IV interim damages and Part V provisional damages. Each Part contains a general description of the existing regime, perceived difficulties with that regime

---

[1]   Fifth Programme of Law Reform,(1991) Law Com. No. 200, Item 11.

[2]   See Report on Personal Injury Litigation - Assessment of Damages,(1973) Law Com. No.56.

[3]   See para. 3.1 and Part III generally for a full description of a structured settlement.

and an examination of the options for reform. Part VI gathers together our provisional conclusions and summarises the consultation issues.

1.4   The publication of this paper is taking place contemporaneously with the carrying out of empirical research which we have commissioned to provide a statistical base for the general damages review. A survey of a representative sample of accident victims who have received damages either through negotiated settlements or pursuant to a court judgment is being undertaken to discover their experiences of, and attitudes to, a range of issues which are fundamental to damages law. Since the announcement of the damages review, the Commission has made contact with, and been contacted by, numerous groups and bodies with an interest in the subject matter, including the Law Society, the Association of Personal Injury Lawyers, Frenkel Topping Structured Settlements, the Departments of Health and Social Security, the Inland Revenue and the Association of British Insurers. The Commission also organised a conference in March 1992 on *Compensation for Personal Injuries - Prospects for the Future* together with the Torts group of the Society of Public Teachers of Law and the Faculty of Law at the University of Manchester. This paper in part draws on the information and preliminary views made known to us by such groups and at the conference, but is intended to stimulate responses and comment from *all* interested parties. Those responses and the relevant statistical data generated by the empirical study will be used to formulate our policy and the recommendations we shall make when we publish our report. We plan to follow this approach when considering other aspects of damages, although later consultation papers may be able to make use of statistical data which is available prior to the date of publication.

1.5   The Commission is most grateful to Roger Bowles of the University of Bath who prepared a paper on the economic background.

PART II

LUMP SUM DAMAGES

Introduction

2.1   Damages in a tort action invariably take the form of a lump sum divided into special damages (for past pecuniary loss) and general damages (for future pecuniary loss including loss of earning capacity and the cost of future care, and non-pecuniary loss whenever occurring such as pain and suffering and loss of amenity).[1] The commonly espoused purpose of these damages is restitutio in integrum - that the plaintiff be restored, as far as is possible in money terms, to the position occupied prior to the accident.[2] This is done by a 'lump sum', that is, a once-and-for-all assessment paid in the form of a single sum.[3] However, this is not self-evidently the ideal form of damages and it is said that the persistence of the lump sum is largely the product of history and inertia.[4] Originally at common law all issues of fact, including the question of damages, were determined by juries. Juries could not be expected to determine exact or even approximate awards (either on a satisfaction, or later, on a loss basis), and therefore their guesses became fossilized in the form of the lump sum. A second reason for the persistence of the once-and-for-all payment is the consistent importance the common law has attached to the need to achieve finality in litigation. Thirdly, it was not previously possible to realise a periodic payment system in practice.[5] Finally, the lump sums claimed have previously been comparatively modest, but this situation has been altered by technological developments which now allow

---

[1]   See *Atiyah's Accidents, Compensation and the Law* (4th ed., 1987),(ed. Cane), p.150 and p. 164; Report of the Royal Commission on Civil Liability and Compensation for Personal Injury [Chairman Lord Pearson],(1978) Cmnd. 7054, vol. 1, p. 121 (hereafter referred to as the *Pearson Report*).

[2]   The *Pearson Report*, vol 1, p. 362, para. 1717.

[3]   See Damages for Personal Injury,(1991), Law Reform Commissioner of Tasmania, Report No. 67, p. 11 (hereafter referred to as *Tasmania Report No. 67*).

[4]   See Gordon Bale, "Encouraging the Hearse Horse Not to Snicker : A Tort Fund Providing Variable Periodic Payments for Pecuniary Loss", in Steel and Rodgers-Magnet (eds), *Issues in Tort Law* (1983), p. 91, at p. 93, and the references therein contained; also, *Tasmania Report No. 67*, p. 11.

[5]   Richard Lewis, "Pensions Replace Lump Sum Damages : Are Structured Settlements the Most Important Reform of Tort in Modern Times?", (1988) 15(4) J. Law. Soc. 392, at p. 397 (hereafter called "Pensions Replace Lump Sum Damages").

intensive assessment of a patient's care needs, and by the use by parties of ever-more sophisticated techniques for loss assessment generally.[6]

2.2   The Pearson Commission noted and rejected the tendency to take it for granted that only a one-off lump sum constitutes acceptable compensation.[7] Increasing acknowledgment of the deficiencies of the lump sum award and the growth in size of claims have combined to change the focus in some cases to alternative forms of payment of damages. This paper is primarily concerned with three such alternatives but before turning to examine those, the advantages and disadvantages of the lump sum will be considered.

The Advantages of the Lump Sum Award

2.3   The fact that lump sum awards bring finality to litigation has already been mentioned. Such finality creates a degree of certainty where there has been uncertainty and allows all parties involved to look to the future instead of the past. The plaintiff can devote full energy to rehabilitation and the defendant (usually an insurer) can close the file and accurately assess all costs. Premiums can be adjusted and policy cover altered if necessary, such decisions informing the public of the true costs of risk-spreading. The administrative resources of the justice system are released for the use of the parties next in line. The lump sum payment is simple and does not need to be policed because there is no need for the plaintiff to be monitored. All cost and expense associated with the dispute cease. The plaintiff is also protected from the possibility of the defendant later becoming insolvent. The state, the public, insurers and individual plaintiffs and defendants have a legitimate interest in such certainty and finality of litigation.[8]

2.4   The fact that lump sums give plaintiffs complete freedom of choice is regarded as just as important. This derives from Western liberal tradition which holds that the individual should be able to pursue any project of endeavour (or indeed, lack of endeavour) so long as there is occasioned no harm to others.[9] Therefore it is seen as advantageous to plaintiffs, awarded perhaps very large sums in damages, to be able to deal with those sums exactly as they wish. While this view recognises that a skilful investor could do extremely well, it accepts and indeed attaches

---

[6]   The *Pearson Report*, vol.1, p. 26, para.82.

[7]   The *Pearson Report*, vol.1, p. 47, para. 178. See also J.Fleming,"Damages : Capital or Rent?" (1969) 19 U. Toronto L.J. 295; Donald Harris, *Remedies in Contract and Tort* (1988), pp. 275-277.

[8]   The *Pearson Report*, vol.1, p. 122, para. 560; and the minority opinion, vol.1, paras. 615-630.

[9]   J.S. Mill, *On Liberty* (1859), The Thinkers Library, 1929, p.11.

importance to the idea that a person should also be quite free to be unskilful, negligent or even a non-investor.[10]

2.5   Further, changes in the circumstances of a plaintiff following settlement can to some degree be met by a lump sum. The form of payment gives the plaintiff the option of calling upon the undissipated capital should unforeseen events create a new and special need.[11] Financial autonomy could also be seen as having a psychological effect in helping restore the confidence of accident victims who perceive and experience a loss of control over their lives.

2.6   A final argument which could be made for the lump sum is that in keeping the focus of negotiations on the full entitlement at law, it also makes plaintiffs aware of their full bargaining power. Because the basic rule is that damages are assessed once and for all, and the plaintiff does not get 'another bite at the cherry', the claim has to be comprehensive if there is to be restitutio in integrum.

The Disadvantages of the Lump Sum Award

Introduction

2.7   The most forceful criticism of the lump sum is that even where the loss to the plaintiff is capable of being expressed in pecuniary terms the award does not in fact accurately replace what has been lost. The tort system offers the full compensation implicit in restitutio in integrum. Apart from symbolically compensating pain and lost pleasures in money terms, it also promises that lost earnings, out of pocket expenses, and possible ill-effects of the injury such as medical complications and loss of marriage or employment prospects will be recoverable.[12] All reasonable future medical and nursing expenses are also recoverable. The difficulty with a lump sum for general damages[13] is that "all future contingencies must be crudely translated into a present value"[14] despite awareness that uncertainty as to the future may mean that the present value is seriously inaccurate.

---

[10]   The *Pearson Report*, vol.1, p. 123, para. 561.

[11]   David Allen, "Structured Settlements", (1988) 104 L.Q.R. 448, at pp. 457-8.

[12]   *Atiyah's Accidents, Compensation and the Law* (4th ed., 1987), (ed. Cane), p. 162.

[13]   Non-pecuniary loss valuation is not dependent upon future contingencies and therefore seems appropriately paid in a lump sum. We are examining non-pecuniary loss as part of this review and will be publishing a consultation paper on that topic.

[14]   D. Harris, *Remedies in Contract and Tort* (1988), p. 276.

2.8   Secondly, it is said that lump sums leave plaintiffs and the state exposed to the risk that the fund will be dissipated. Thirdly, it is said that lump sums add to costs, cause delay and hinder rather than aid rehabilitation. Finally, there may be tax and inflation disadvantages. We set out the specific problems below, but feel able to make provisional recommendations in relation to the first problem only. The discussion in Parts III, IV and V adverts to the other difficulties mentioned in this Part and possible solutions to them.

The uncertain future

(a) The multiplier/multiplicand method of assessment

(i) Introduction

2.9   One dimension to the 'uncertain future' problem is the need for the court in estimating pecuniary loss to make 'guesstimates' of both the future general financial situation and the plaintiff's future. The judicial approach to the quantification of loss entails, broadly speaking, an identification of the net annual loss (the multiplicand), and the number of years for which the loss will last (the multiplier). The multiplicand is adjusted for any prospect of increased earnings whilst the multiplier is scaled down to reflect the contingencies of life and the fact that the money will be available to the plaintiff sooner under a lump sum award than it would otherwise have been, allowing the plaintiff to invest the money to produce a positive real return during the years of the loss. It is the choice of multiplier which is generally the more difficult part of the calculation. Defendants wish the multiplier to be as low as possible whilst plaintiffs wish the reverse. The court often has to make judgments about the likelihood of contingencies occurring in deciding whether to downrate the multiplier, and to take a view on the discount to be made because the lump sum is receivable in advance. An alternative approach, considered below,[15] is an actuarial one using combined annuity and life expectation tables.

2.10   The Law Commission has previously summarised the prevailing judicial attitude as follows:[16]

> (a) the use of the multiplier has been, remains and should continue to remain, the ordinary, the best and the most satisfactory method of assessing the value of a number of future annual sums both in regard to claims for lost dependency under the Fatal Accidents Acts and claims for future loss of earnings or future expenses;

---

[15]   See paras. 2.16 ff.

[16]   (1973) Law Com. No. 56, p. 61, para. 222.

(b) the actuarial method of calculation, whether from expert evidence or from tables, continues to be technically admissible and technically relevant but its usefulness is confined, except perhaps in very unusual cases, to an ancillary means of checking a computation already made by the multiplier method.

2.11   A number of criticisms have been made of the multiplier system as it operates in practice. It seems, for example, that some judges adjust the multiplier downward to take account of the risk of early death even when this has been fully discounted in the determination of the number of years the loss is expected to endure.[17] In addition it seems that the size of the discount made for contingencies may be somewhat arbitrary. Ogus notes[18] that the plaintiff's position may have turned out worse than forecast as well as better and this casts doubt on the wisdom of applying heavy discounts in choosing multipliers.

2.12   The assumption implicit in the discounts applied by the courts in calculating multipliers is that the real rate of return on investment after tax is around 4 to 5%.[19] For this reason courts will usually apply a discount of this amount to the multiplier. We recognise that there are significant practical advantages leading to a saving in court time and costs in applying a conventional discount without evidence being called on the point. However, in practice both nominal and real interest rates fluctuate frequently. Appendix A illustrates the behaviour of interest rates. Table 1 and Figure 1 illustrate the history of real interest rates over the past twenty years. They show interest rates considerably higher, in real terms, in the 1980s as compared with the 1970s because of changes in the inflationary climate (triggered in part by oil prices and monetary policy). These rates are pre-tax rates. Even during the period when interest rates were high the average real rate was only 3.55%. During the 1970s when

---

[17]   See e.g., Sir Gordon Willmer in *Mitchell* v. *Mulholland* (No. 2) [1972] 1 Q.B. 65, 85-6; followed by Waller L.J., in *Auty* v. *N.C.B.* [1985] 1 W.L.R., 784,798, despite the fact that attention was drawn to the matter by the Law Commission in 1971 (*Personal Injury Litigation - Assessment of Damages*, Working Paper No. 41, para. 164, n.129). See also *Kemp and Kemp. The Quantum of Damages*, vol.1, at 8-005.

[18]   *The Law of Damages* (1973), p. 189.

[19]   *Cookson* v. *Knowles* [1979] A.C. 566, *per* Lord Diplock, 571 (in times of stable currency). No account appears to be taken of capital gains in the investments assumed to be made to produce the return. Lord Diplock later adopted a rate of 2% at a time of rampant inflation in *Wright* v. *British Railways Board* [1983] 2 A.C. 773, 783. However, that case was concerned with the appropriate interest rates for non-economic loss. *Roberts* v. *Johnstone* [1989] Q.B. 878, subsequently established the use of a rate of 2% when compensating for future pecuniary loss such as the forced acquisition of a capital asset, in this case a house, where the 2% was felt appropriate to take account of increase in value. However, in cases of all other pecuniary loss, the conventional rate of 4 to 5% is applied. See *Kemp and Kemp*, vol. 1, ch. 7, pp. 7001-7023. We will refer to a rate of 4.5% throughout for ease of reference.

much of the earlier debate about multipliers took place, the rate was actually negative, suggesting that multipliers should have been considerably higher than those actually used in practice. Figure 2 in Appendix A gives a more detailed view of (nominal) interest rates since 1990. It shows the relatively rapid changes which can take place over a short time. It also shows that the appropriate discount rate should vary according to the state of the financial markets.[20] For example, with a loss stretching over 25 years the multiplier with a discount based on a 4.5% real rate of return is 15, but, applying a discount based on a real rate of 2%, it increases to 20.

2.13 The insurance market is now able to put a price on a complex set of annuities which will be sensitive to conditions in financial markets and will reflect both present interest rates on relevant financial instruments and the market's expectation as to future interest rates as implied in the relative rates available on investments of different duration. Only by chance, and on occasion, will the figure for the real rate of interest be the 4.5% assumed by the courts. The consequence of the court insisting on a multiplier based on that assumption is that plaintiffs will find themselves well or harshly treated (in terms of their capacity to buy appropriate annuities) depending on where market rates of interest rest at the time of the award.

2.14 Some of the difficulties faced by the judiciary in applying the multiplier approach can be illustrated by reference to *Lim* v. *Camden Health Authority*[21]. Lord Scarman, discussing the element of the award in respect of future care, referred to the remarks of the judge[22] :

> "Her expectation of life, according to the tables, will be in the order of a further 37 years. In this case I must make a substantial discount because of the accelerated payment, some reduction for the contingency that she will not reach the average age, some reduction to allow for the purely domestic element, and some increase for prospective inflation. Balancing these elements as best I can, I find the appropriate multiplier for the period of future care in England to be 11."[23]

---

[20] In particular the relative movement of domestic inflation and interest rates. Thus, if inflation falls from 6% per annum to 4% while interest rates remain steady at 10%, the real interest rate will rise from 4% to 6%. The result is that the real interest rate can and does move quite rapidly with significant repercussions for the cost of buying an annuity and thus for the plaintiff about to be awarded a lump sum of damages.

[21] [1980] A.C. 174. For comment see David Kemp Q.C., "The Assessment of Damages for Future Pecuniary Loss in Personal Injury Claims", (1984) 3 C.J.Q. 120 pp. 126-127.

[22] *Lim* v. *Camden Health Authority* [1980] A.C. 174, 195H-196B.

[23] [1979] Q.B. 196, 203.

Lord Scarman pointed out that adjustment for the 'domestic element' is normally made through the multiplicand rather than the multiplier and accordingly made an adjustment. He also confirmed that damages are to be assessed without regard to future inflation, unless exceptional circumstances exist. He made a further adjustment for the fact that under the award "capital as well as the income arising is to be available for meeting the cost of care",[24] and arrived at a multiplier of 12.

2.15   The extent of the reduction for the contingency of not reaching the average age was not discussed in explicit, numerical terms. Indeed, it is difficult to ascertain very clearly what view was taken about survival. In his discussion of loss of future earnings and pension at a later part of the judgment Lord Scarman made the following observations:

> "Dr Lim's expectation of life after her injury is substantially as it was before her injury. Nevertheless... the contingency of an earlier death is plainly more likely after than it was before her injury."[25]

In the event, Lord Scarman upheld the judge's award of a multiplier of 14 for loss of future earnings. Given that at the date of trial (December 1977) the plaintiff was aged 40 and thus could have expected to work for a further 20 years, the multiplier of 14 falls within the discount bracket of 4 to 5% suggested by Lord Diplock. A heavy discount of pension rights was also upheld by Lord Scarman, suggesting an implicit assumption that Dr Lim faced a high probability of premature death but only once she had reached retirement age. It is not easy to discern why the multiplier for loss of future earnings should, in this particular case, exceed the multiplier for the cost of future care. The other observation which may be made, admittedly with the benefit of hindsight, is that a doctor highly regarded as a senior registrar in psychiatry in 1977 would have had a high expectation of early appointment to a position as consultant. By 1992, at the age of 55, the same doctor was likely to have been earning a great deal more in real terms than the amount assumed by the courts in Dr Lim's case.

(ii) The actuarial approach

2.16   Much of the controversy surrounding the multiplier has centred on its relation with actuarial evidence. In making allowance for the chances and contingencies of life, it is appropriate to adjust the multiplier for the possibility that the loss may not continue over the projected time horizon because the plaintiff may die in the meantime. Death is not the only

---

[24]   *Lim v. Camden Health Authority* [1980] A.C. 174, 196C.

[25]   *Ibid.* As to allowance for inflation, see para. 2.42 below.

contingency to consider but it is usually the most important. One way of incorporating the contingency of death is to use a table giving survival probabilities. These probabilities are age and sex specific. A male worker aged 37 might have expected to work for 28 years until the age of 65, but the multiplier has to be revised to take account of the prospects of death before that age. When the award of damages is being made, the expected loss in a future year is calculated as the annual loss multiplied by a factor reflecting the probability that the man will still be alive in that year. The probability of survival will decrease through time and thus an ever smaller sum will fall to be discounted. Actuarial tables of multipliers are prepared with these contingencies incorporated. There are different tables for men and women to reflect variations in retirement age and mortality rates between the sexes. Such tables are sometimes referred to in judgments, for example in *Lim's case*.

2.17 Actuaries have developed expertise in calculating survival probabilities for classes of individuals with particular characteristics. The courts have often argued that such an approach is conjectural,[26] that they are dealing with a single individual rather than a class of individuals and that they are very experienced in estimating the contingencies relevant to that person. This criticism of an actuarial approach may be unfair. Although many of the published actuarial tables are based on data for the whole population, there is nothing to prevent a more detailed analysis of an individual's position. Indeed, if it is sought to buy a substantial annuity with settlement funds, the life office will require a lot of detailed information about the plaintiff's health status and prognosis for actuarial scrutiny before agreeing terms.

2.18 The Law Commission has previously criticised the ruling of the House of Lords in *Taylor* v. *O'Connor*[27] under which the "multiplier" approach was to be regarded as the normal and primary method of assessment.[28] We concluded then that a new approach was desirable giving greater weight to the acceptability of actuarial evidence and freeing the courts from the inhibiting influence of *Taylor* v. *O'Connor* and the further ruling of the Court of Appeal in *Mitchell* v. *Mulholland* (No.2).[29] We

---

26 *Auty* v. *N.C.B.* [1985] 1 W.L.R. 784, *per Oliver L.J.*, 800-801 (it is only a little more likely to be accurate than the predictions of an astrologer); *Taylor* v. *O'Connor* [1971] A.C. 115, 140G (a false appearance of accuracy and precision in a sphere where conjectural assessments have to play a large part). Cf. D. Harris, *Remedies in Contract and Tort* (1988), p. 270.

27 [1971] A.C. 115.

28 Personal Injury Litigation - Assessment of Damages (1971), (hereafter W.P. 41 (one of the working papers which led to Law Com No. 56) at para. 162.

29 [1972] 1 Q.B. 65, affirmed in *Auty* v. *N.C.B* [1985] 1 W.L.R. 784. In *Spiers* v. *Halliday*, *The Times*, 30 June 1984, the court refused to have regard to actuarial tables without evidence of their accuracy.

recommended legislation to promote the use of actuarial evidence.[30] This recommendation was not implemented, but another,[31] that official actuarial tables be prepared, has led to the publication by the Government Actuary's Department of the *Actuarial Tables with Explanatory Notes for use in Personal Injury and Fatal Accident Cases*, often referred to as "the Ogden Tables".[32] The explanatory notes to the tables make it clear that they do not eliminate the need for actuarial evidence in absolutely all cases but could do so in many. In the recent Scottish case of *O'Brien's Curator Bonis* v. *British Steel plc*[33] the First Division held that there was no reason why judicial notice should not be taken of the Ogden Tables, including the report of the working party, and that it could be assumed that the calculations which they reflect are arithmetically accurate. An appeal by the defendants to the House of Lords was withdrawn. However, in England and Wales, in the absence of legislation, an actuary has to be called to prove the Ogden tables if they are to be used in evidence.

(iii) The European position

2.19   The majority of European countries make use of actuarial tables for future loss claims and calculations. The countries are: Belgium, France, Italy, the Netherlands, Germany, which uses a 3.5-5.0% discount rate, Sweden, which uses a 6.5% discount rate for 10 years and 4.0% thereafter, and Switzerland, where the tables have been used since last century, with a current discount rate of 3.5%. In Denmark, Norway and Spain there is no obligation to use actuarial tables, though tables have been published in Spain.[34]

---

[30]   (1973) Law Com. No. 56, p. 63, para. 230.

[31]   arising from an Inter-Professional Working Party chaired by Sir Michael Ogden QC, and set up in late 1982.

[32]   The Tables take no account of risks other than mortality, such as permanent ill- health leading to loss of employment, redundancy and early retirement (see Ogden Tables, HMSO, 1984, reprinted in *Kemp & Kemp*, vol. 1, 8-029). However, we understand that work is under way to extend the allowance made in the Tables for other risks, and to correct other anomalies. It is intended that the results of such work will eventually be published as an Addendum to the Tables. (Interview with Sir Michael Ogden Q.C., 15 July 1992).

[33]   [1991] S.L.T. 477.

[34]   See C.N. McEachran, Q.C., "*O'Brien's C.B* v. *British Steel*. A postscript on Claims for Future Services, Actuarial Tables and the European Dimension", (1992) 15 S.L.T. 139.

(iv) Change in the financial background

2.20 Since the Law Commission and the Pearson Commission reported there has been an important change which is relevant to the question of the method to be used to estimate future loss. In 1981 the UK Government began to issue Index-Linked Government Securities ("ILGS"). Both the coupon (in effect, the interest rate) and the redemption value of these bonds are adjusted for movements in the Retail Price Index. This enables insurance companies to offer annuities and other financial instruments which provide great flexibility in their capacity to produce a wide variety of future income profiles. It appears that financial markets are now able to offer securities providing full protection against inflation over any required time span. Essentially, they appear able to put an accurate present price on a loss extending over a period by offering riskless, inflation-proof securities.

(v) Provisional conclusions

2.21 We believe, as we did in 1973, in the value of actuarial methods of assessing future loss. Our provisional conclusion is that actuarial methods should be given greater prominence in the awarding of lump sums. However, it is important to bear in mind that despite elaborate calculations concerning mortality, the assessment of loss could be falsified by application of an inappropriate discount rate. The present interest rate and projections of its future movements are both subject to continuous adjustment. But the presumption is that the court will always abide by its figure of 4.5% as appropriate in determining the discount. Insurance companies do not take decisions based on such simplistic assumptions. Annuities involve such companies in making a promise to make payments over a long period of time on the basis of more sophisticated methods of predicting future interest rates and hedging the risk of interest rate movements. We therefore believe that the need for actuarial methods to be given greater prominence goes hand in hand with the need for more thought to be given to the choice of the appropriate discount rate when selecting multipliers in individual cases. This becomes even more important when we note the effects of taxation at paragraphs 2.37-2.41 below.

2.22 The Ogden Tables deal with the issue of inflation by assuming that the plaintiff will invest the damages award in Index-Linked Government Securities. The advent of those securities in 1981 substantially strengthens the case for making greater use of actuarial evidence. The multipliers in the Ogden Tables can be chosen by reference to the rate of discount corresponding to the yield on such stocks at the date of assessment. The value of actuarial evidence is also supported by the experience of structured settlements and the implications of their wider use, since they are based on complex actuarial calculations and predictions.[35] Accordingly, subject to the views of consultees, we believe that the time has come to encourage the general use of these tables by legislation.[36] We invite views on the extent to which courts should use actuarial evidence.

(vi) A radical approach

2.23 We are, however, inclined to go further. The multiplier approach is very flexible in that it can incorporate virtually any assumption about 'contingencies and chances', and about interest rates. However, the use of the multiplier system seems to us to be inappropriate unless use is also made of the most up-to-date information. Because we believe that to make complex assumptions about mortality rates would not lead to the most accurate assessment of damages so long as very crude assumptions about interest rates are made, our provisional view is that courts should make more use of information from the financial markets in discounting lump sums to take account of the fact that they are paid today. One way of doing this would be if courts were able to refer to the rate of return on Index-Linked Government Securities ("ILGS") to establish an appropriate rate of discount.[37] The aim would be to reflect the best market opinion as to what real interest rates will be. Because the quoted stocks show a range of yields, it might be appropriate for the court to consider published yields on a basket of ILGS for a set period, for example a month. An alternative method might be to require expert evidence analysing this data to be put before the court by the parties. The question upon which we seek the views of consultees is whether it is possible to use the return on ILGS as a guide to the appropriate discount. If so, we would welcome advice as to exactly how that could be done and whether it would be a less arbitrary method than reliance on the conventional 4.5%. We also seek the views of consultees as to possible alternatives to ILGS as suitable indicators.

2.24 Such an approach rests on the assumption that ILGS are a permanent feature of the financial market. ILGS have been issued from time to time since 1981, the latest issue being on 12 June 1992 with a redemption date of 2030. We accept that there is no guarantee that the Government will continue to offer such stock. However, it is reasonable to proceed on the basis that they are now an established feature of the market. As long as there are concerns about the rate of inflation and whether or not it can be

---

[35] See also paras. 3.69 and 3.70 below.

[36] Judges will still have to adjust the multipliers derived from the Ogden Tables to account for the extra contingencies not covered. However, we expect the process of improvement and refinement of the Tables to continue, and indeed to be boosted by the effects of formalisation.

[37] See *Kemp & Kemp*, vol.1, 7-015.

controlled, there will be a perceived need for such stock. Further, it is likely that insurance companies will maintain demand for ILGS even when inflation is low since the purchase of the stock allows them to hedge their long term liabilities. If, however, there are significant doubts about our assumptions, flexibility could be preserved in any legislation establishing the rule as to the use of this evidence. Should ILGS cease to be available, Rules of Court could allow for a suitable replacement to be specified. Obviously if ILGS no longer exist and no alternative is specified, judges will not be required to take account of such evidence.

2.25 If this approach is possible, it would be necessary to decide how much weight should be given to such evidence. There could be a mandatory legislative direction requiring that notice be taken of the relevant evidence in every case. Alternatively, legislation could require that where a decision is made to adopt a rate of discount different from that suggested by reference to a test of the sort we have outlined above, the court must give reasons for its decision. Subject to the views of consultees, our provisional view is that, if it is possible to use the rate of return to determine the appropriate discount, the first option is preferable. If a formula based on the rate of return on ILGS is more reliable than assuming a conventional rate of 4.5% it should be used. If it is not, it should not be used.

2.26 There is another and possibly simpler way of using the financial markets to assist in the determination of awards. The developments in the tax treatment of annuities and availability of Index-Linked Government Securities could be taken together as the basis for the assessment of damages generally. The essence of this is that it has become possible, if not desirable, to decouple the court's role in identifying the loss from its role in commuting the loss into a single lump sum of damages. The financial markets have the capacity to translate a specified income replacement stream into a capital sum and vice versa. The increasing sophistication of financial markets and the wider range of products they are able to offer since the advent of ILGS is a substantial resource and one which could be much more effectively utilised by the courts. The use of such expertise offers a number of advantages and is immune from much of the criticism of the present multiplier system. It would simplify the calculations the court has to do and reduce the number and variety of factors being loaded into the multiplier. The court would be able to focus its energies on identifying the extent of annual loss and the time horizon over which loss is expected.

2.27 On this approach the court would reach a view as to the annual loss and the number of years over which the loss could be expected to continue. The court would not identify a multiplier as in the present system. Instead, it would, having designated an income stream for replacement, require evidence to be adduced of the capital cost of an appropriate bundle of securities. This capital cost could then be expressed, if required, as a lump sum. It would remain possible for the plaintiff to opt for the lump sum in preference to the bundle of annuities identified by the court's adviser. It would be possible to specify very precisely the nature of the income stream to be replaced. It could be a steadily escalating (or declining) annual sum; the sum could be fully indexed against the RPI; there could be a series of overlapping policies; and the policies could run for a fixed term or for the life of the plaintiff (or the beneficiary). The question of evidence again arises. We do not see this suggestion as being effective unless reliance on the expert evidence is mandatory.

2.28   We do not express a view as to these further possibilities but invite comment on their desirability and practicality. One important question which must be answered is how account would be taken of contingencies which cannot be allowed for in the multiplicand. These include the possibility of redundancy and time off work for illness. Judges presently take account of these by reducing the multiplier, a process which is not possible if the court no longer identifies a multiplier. One solution could be to allow the judge to adjust the final financial package, by reducing a particular income stream, or rounding down the lump sum as expressed. Although by no means ideal, this may not greatly differ from what currently occurs. However, it would not be desirable if it destroyed the advantages of the financial package. We seek comment on this proposition, the difficulty outlined and any other difficulties foreseen.

(b) Chance and forecast cases

2.29   The other dimension to the 'uncertain future' problem has already been examined by this Commission. We previously analysed a significant problem in assessing future pecuniary loss by describing two types of cases: **chance** cases and **forecast** cases.[38] The **chance** case is one where the injury apparent at trial is later exacerbated by catastrophe, for example, epilepsy or cancer. In seeking to make allowance for such inestimable possibilities, all that can be done is to rely on percentage estimates of the event actually taking place. However, if for example there is a 10% chance of the catastrophe and the damages are calculated as if it has happened, but are reduced to take account of the percentage chance of its not happening, there can never be compensation for the loss actually suffered. If the event happens, the plaintiff has been under-compensated and the defendant has received a windfall. If the event does not take place, the defendant has paid too much, and the plaintiff has received the windfall.[39]

---

[38]   (1973) Law Com. No. 56, p. 64.

[39]   The Law Commission noted that justice might be done if the sum awarded was sufficient to permit the plaintiff to take out a suitable insurance policy, but doubted whether such policies, geared to the individual circumstances of each case, would be available on the insurance market.(1973) Law Com. No. 56, p. 64, paras. 233 and 234.

2.30   The **forecast** case is one where an element of the damages award depends on the medical prognosis being correct. This may relate either to duration of incapacity and affect the determination of necessity for future care, to loss of earning capacity, or to the development of an incapacity connected to the injury, with similar effect. A correct prognosis will ensure sufficient damages are awarded but, while in contrast to the chance case the possibility of accuracy at least exists, there are still no guarantees.[40]

The risk of dissipation

2.31   The argument next advanced with considerable force against the lump sum award is that plaintiffs are exposed to significant risks that the fund will be dissipated leaving them destitute and dependent on state funds for survival. The corollary of the freedom of individuals to spend as they are inclined is having to bear the consequences of unwise or simply naive investment, or of over-generosity based on perceived familial obligation.[41] It has also been observed that, understandably, many injured claimants simply want to 'buy' friendship.[42] Related to this is the suggestion that the plaintiff will spend at a more rapid rate than the court predicts and will thus fail to save for the future.[43] This argument often makes reference to 'the unsophisticated investor' receiving sums out of all proportion to previous experience and falling prey to a 'pools-win' syndrome as a result.

2.32   How far these contentions about dissipation are true remains in dispute. The empirical study most often referred to in the literature and by practitioners is that reportedly carried out by the American life insurance industry in the late 1970s[44] stating that 25% of award recipients had

---

[40]   An informal survey maintained by the Master of the Court of Protection since 1988 reveals that in some of the personal injury cases dealt with the medical prognosis was substantially incorrect. The mistakes covered forecasts as to recovery of mental capacity, expectation of life, and ability to return to employment; in general what proved to be an unrealistically pessimistic view was taken. Damages based on such prognoses would both overcompensate and undercompensate.

[41]   *Atiyah's Accidents, Compensation and the Law* (4th ed., 1987), (ed. Cane), p. 159; R. Lewis, "Pensions Replace Lump Sum Damages", (1988) 15, J. Law. Soc. 392, p. 398.

[42]   Comment in letter from McKellar Structured Settlements of Ontario, Canada dated 27 May 1992. This firm was the first company to specialise in structured settlements in Canada, and is currently the largest seller of structures in that country.

[43]   *Atiyah's Accidents, Compensation and the Law* (4th ed., 1987), (ed. Cane), pp. 159-160.

[44]   Edwin G. Upenieks correctly notes in "Structured Settlements: Are They Here to Stay?", (1982) 3 *Advocates Quarterly* (1982) 393, at p. 406, n. 59, that the interesting feature of this study is that the actual survey cannot be found, only references to sources in which it has been cited. For example, see 1987) Manitoba Law Reform Commission No. 68, p. 54, n. 21, *Report on Periodic Payment of Damages for Personal Injury and Death* (hereafter referred to as the *Manitoba Law Reform Commission Report, No. 68*), which also contains references to studies

nothing left of their award at the end of two months, 50% had nothing left at the end of one year, 70% had nothing left after the second year and 90% had nothing left after five years. However, it has been suggested that this study should be treated with caution as there is no indication whether the awards investigated were adequate to last for more than five years to begin with.[45] The Pearson Commission's personal injury survey showed that only 5 % of recipients invested any of their funds.[46] However, most of the sums involved in that survey were very small. A more recent survey carried out in the United Kingdom[47] asked accident victims who received damages about their use of the damages and about the advice which they received on their use. The majority used some or all of the money in a way which sought to preserve the benefit for a considerable period.[48] Although this does not tell us anything about dissipation, it does say something about what people seek to achieve. The survey also concluded that even where larger sums were involved[49] people did not seek professional investment advice about what to do with the money.

2.33   The evidence therefore remains sketchy and anecdotal. We hope our empirical research will shed further light on the question of dissipation of damages awards. The existing evidence is seen as significant to the degree that one head of damages which is increasingly claimed is that of a fee to allow individuals to hire professionals to help them manage their

---

(cont'd) carried out for the Automobile Accident Compensation Committee in British Columbia in 1983, the Pearson Commission, and a 1936 study of vocational rehabilitation and workmen's compensation. See also the Australian examples given by Harold Luntz in *Assessment of Damages for Personal Injury and Death* (3rd ed., 1990), p. 20, n. 28.

[45]   See Christopher J. Bruce, "Four Techniques for Compensating Tort Damages", (1983) 21(1) U.W. Ont.L. Rev. 1, at p. 6, n. 17.

[46]   The *Pearson Report*, vol. 1, p. 123, para. 562.

[47]   The study reported by Harris et al, *Compensation and Support for Illness and Injury* (1984), pp. 121 - 123.

[48]   *Ibid.*, p. 122.

[49]   Damages over £1,000. The median of all 152 settlements in the survey was £500. See p. Harris et al, *ibid.*, 123.

awards effectively.[50] Whatever the reality, it cannot be denied that the risk of dissipation of lump sum awards does exist.[51]

2.34   Since ultimately it is the state and not the individual which bears the consequences of the dissipation of lump sum awards, the question arises whether this justifies intervention by the law. In this, the clash is a direct one between the principles of corrective and distributive justice. Those who see the element of freedom embodied in the lump sum award in a positive light would submit that justice has been done in the individual case and no question of post-misallocation arises as the individual has been put in the position she or he would have been in had the injury not occurred. Those who fear the dissipation of the lump sum would argue that in fact the plaintiff who receives a lump sum is not in the position occupied prior to the accident or injury. Prior to the injury she or he was almost certainly not in possession of a large sum of money but was in receipt of a regular payment of wages or a salary. Although it is recognised that the intention behind a lump sum is that it will be invested to produce amounts equivalent to wages or a salary, because there is no guarantee that this will occur, payment of a lump sum is seen as a misallocation of funds which should have been redistributed over time. Since dissipation would further misallocate funds, intervention to prevent this is justified. Further, the likelihood that the destitute plaintiff will fall back on state support to survive is an additional misallocation of wealth in that the public is in effect forced to pay for the plaintiff's injuries twice over, once in the form of insurance premiums and again in the form of taxes supporting benefits.[52] Finally, although able-bodied citizens who receive a large capital sum are in a position to pauperise themselves just like those awarded lump sums, unlike the accident victim, the able-bodied citizen retains her or his actual earning capacity, and is sifted out of state support where that capacity is intact and jobs are available.[53]

---

[50]   However, if the victim is not a patient within the jurisdiction of the Court of Protection, investment advice costs are not recoverable - see *Francis* v. *Bostock, Kemp and Kemp*, vol. 2, A2-102, at p. 51225. A recent trend has been the appearance of specialist divisions within solicitors firms offering Care Manager services advising on victims' financial affairs following the award of damages. However, the trend does not seem to have continued. (Interview with the Master of the Court of Protection, 15 January 1992).

[51]   See also Samuel A Rea, Jr, "Lump-Sum versus Periodic Damage Awards",(1987) 10 J. Legal Studies 131, at p. 142.

[52]   *Tasmania Report No. 67*, p. 17.

[53]   See Christopher J. Bruce, "Four Techniques for Compensating Tort Damages", (1983) 21(1) U.W. Ont. L. Rev. 1, at p. 8.

Costs, delay and hindrance to rehabilitation

2.35 A third argument made against lump sums is that they add to costs, cause delay, and hinder, rather than aid, rehabilitation.[54] Assessment can only occur once and therefore requires the most accurate medical prognosis possible. This involves waiting for the plaintiff's condition to stabilise, a period of two to three years being typical in serious cases. Rehabilitation may be further delayed by various factors deriving from the fact that damages are in the form of a one-off lump sum. The plaintiff is aware that any improvement in her or his condition will mean a reduction in damages, which may inhibit rehabilitation. However, at the same time, any delay compounds anxiety about the outcome of the trial, during which time the plaintiff may have additional difficulties surviving on social welfare payments. Atiyah refers to this phenomenon as 'compensation neurosis'.[55] It generally ceases after the trial or settlement, and is not conscious malingering, but can clearly interfere with the accurate assessment of damages.

2.36 While delay continues, costs increase, adding further to the anxiety of the plaintiff. It has been observed that at a certain point, this stress becomes intolerable. The plaintiff is then susceptible to settling the claim sooner rather than proceeding to trial, perhaps receiving less than might otherwise have been possible.[56] In the long run these contradictory forces operate to short-change the plaintiff, a situation which is actively exploited by defendants' insurers in negotiation.[57]

Taxation

2.37 Finally, apart from the plaintiff's need to ensure that she or he receives an adequate continuing income from the lump sum received, the tax treatment of damages must be considered. Although the lump sum itself

---

[54] Richard Lewis, "Pensions Replace Lump Sum Damages", (1988) 15 J. Law. Soc. 392, at p. 399.

[55] *Atiyah's Accidents, Compensation and the Law* (4th ed., 1987), (ed. Cane), p. 151.

[56] Harris et al, found that 99 % of claims started were concluded by means of a negotiated settlement. The study also revealed that two-thirds of cases where settlement is reached are concluded on the basis of the first offer made by the defendant's insurers: *Compensation and Support for Illness and Injury* (1984), pp. 93-104. Also referred to in Hazel Genn, *Hard Bargaining. Out of Court Settlement in Personal Injury Actions* (1987), preface and p. 13.

[57] H. Genn, *Hard Bargaining*, (1987), ch. 6.

is not subject to tax,[58] any investment income derived from it is subject to tax in the normal way.[59] We have, however, noted that payments received under a structured settlement may not be subject to tax. This is discussed at paragraphs 3.9-3.13 below.

2.38 The question of taxation in relation to lump sum damages bears closer scrutiny. In *British Transport Commission* v. *Gourley*[60] the House of Lords, overruling earlier cases, held that in calculating damages for loss of earnings, account must be taken of the tax which would have been payable upon them. Such damages were awarded as compensation, and the amount must be determined by the application of reasonable common sense, taking into account all matters which might have affected the plaintiff's tax liability. The effect of the *Gourley* rule is that all personal injury compensation for loss of earnings is paid net and is not taxed. Therefore, if the loss is calculated at £100,000, the sum payable by the defendant to a basic rate taxpayer will be £75,000. The principle of restitutio in integrum is preserved since the plaintiff has not been overcompensated. However, the state does not pursue the defendant for the £25,000 representing the tax which would have been paid had the plaintiff not been injured.[61]

2.39 It has been suggested that the *Gourley* rule has the effect of providing a fiscal subsidy to those who are negligent, since the burden of the loss of the tax which the plaintiff would have paid is borne by taxpayers in general.[62] Thus, the deterrent effect of imposing tort liability is diminished. The Law Commission previously considered this criticism[63] but recommended no change, emphasising that there was no reason why someone who has lost a net sum should receive a gross sum. On consultation there was little dissent from this view. It was also noted that

---

[58] Taxation of Chargeable Gains Act 1992, s. 51(2): "It is hereby declared that sums obtained by way of compensation or damages for any wrong or injury suffered by an individual in his person or in his profession or vocation are not chargeable gains."

[59] Income and Corporation Taxes Act 1988, s. 656. Prior to 1984, when investment income was subject to an investment income surcharge, income from a lump sum payment could, when combined with income from other sources, take the plaintiff into what was arguably an inappropriate tax bracket.

[60] [1956] A.C. 185.

[61] The apparent gain to defendant employers from the *Gourley* rule (where, at a 25% tax rate, there is only three quarters of the apparent saving) may be illusory. If the employer has to employ a substitute employee at the same wage, anything paid by way of damages (ignoring the effect of insurance) is pure loss. This would not, of course, apply to non-employer defendants.

[62] W. Bishop and J. Kay, "Taxation and Damages : The Rule in Gourley's Case", (1987) 103 L.Q.R. 211, at p. 220, and D. Harris, *Remedies in Contract and Tort* (1988), p. 265.

[63] (1973) Law Com. No. 56, p. 14, paras. 49-52.

such a change would entail the Commission advising that damages for personal injuries should be subject to tax in the hands of the plaintiff although such damages had been expressly exempted from taxation by the legislature.[64] We are of the provisional view that the reasoning of the Commission is still sound, but seek consultees' views.

2.40 A situation described as "*Gourley* in reverse"[65] occurs where the lump sum or part of it is invested, so that interest is earned on the income, but the interest itself attracts tax. In *Taylor* v. *O'Connor*[66] Lord Reid noted that lump sums were intended to be prudently invested and used up gradually. Interest and damages together should be adequate to last out the period required.[67] However, where an annuity was purchased for example, although part of each annual payment would be a return on capital and not taxable, that part which was truly income would bear tax. Therefore the amount available to the plaintiff to spend would fall short by the amount of the tax paid. In such a case it could be said the plaintiff has been taxed twice. Here, taking account of the possible incidence of tax justified an increase in the award either by an increase in the multiplier or in the figure of the annual loss, the multiplicand. This practice was followed in the Court of Appeal in *Thomas* v. *Wignall*[68], but that case was overruled by the House of Lords in *Hodgson* v. *Trapp*,[69] and the practice of allowing for tax restricted to very exceptional circumstances where there is positive evidence that justice requires it. Lord Oliver there observed, that "the incidence of taxation in the future should ordinarily be assumed to be satisfactorily taken care of in the conventional assumption of an interest rate applicable to a stable currency and the selection of a multiplier appropriate to that rate"[70].

2.41 Our examination at paragraphs 2.12, 2.13 and 2.21 above of the conventional assumption referred to by Lord Oliver must call such reasoning into question. The suggestions we make as to actuarial methods and the use of evidence from the financial markets at paragraphs 2.21 to 2.28 would allow taxation to be taken into account to a degree in establishing more accurate multipliers. The suggestion we make at

---

[64] See Kerridge, "The Taxation of Emoluments from Offices and Employments",(1992) 108 L.Q.R. 433, for a recent formulation of this argument.

[65] *Kemp and Kemp*, vol. 1, 9-031.

[66] [1971] A.C. 115.

[67] *Ibid.*, 128.

[68] [1987] Q.B. 1098.

[69] [1989] A.C. 807.

[70] *Ibid.*, 835B.

paragraphs 3.92 to 3.97 below as to an alteration to the tax regime presently applying to structured settlements would, we suggest, remove the difficulty altogether. We invite comment on this analysis.

Inflation

2.42 In *Auty* v. *N. C. B.* [71] the Court of Appeal affirmed the rule that inflation should not affect the assessment of compensation in personal injury cases. Thus, inflation is to be ignored. Again, we note that our proposals outlined at paragraphs 2.21 to 2.28 would mean that account would necessarily be taken of inflation through the use of actuarial evidence and the assessment through the financial markets of the real rate of return on Index-Linked Government Securities. We invite comment on this proposition.

---

[71]   [1985] 1 W.L.R. 784.

PART III

STRUCTURED SETTLEMENTS

Introduction

3.1   The structured settlement provides an alternative form of damages to the lump sum award.   Structured settlements have developed in the United Kingdom without legislative assistance as a result of their tax free status. They usually consist of an initial lump sum partial payment and an annuity or series of annuities.   The initial lump sum tends to represent an award for past pain and suffering and costs and expenses already incurred.   The defendant uses the balance of the award to purchase the annuity or annuities from a life insurance company.   The payments made under the annuities become a pension for the plaintiff, with payments usually lasting for life or a specified term, whichever is the longer.[1]   The flexibility of the structure is such that any number of annuities, linked to the plaintiff's life and geared to projected future needs, can be purchased.   Thus, a deferred annuity could commence at a pre-determined future date, for example, to provide for university education.   Another annuity could be a step annuity which pays out lump sums every four to five years to cater for replacement of capital items throughout the lifetime of the plaintiff. A temporary annuity could provide resources during the minority of a child. Most annuities tend to be index-linked.   Because future needs can never be fixed and because, once settled, the structure cannot be altered, a contingency fund is also a typical part of the package.   At present, in the United Kingdom, structures are agreed voluntarily between the parties[2]. There has been intense interest in these settlements, with an unfortunate

---

[1]   The rationale behind a structure lasting beyond the lifetime of the plaintiff is unclear. The explanations given for such an arrangement include returning at least the price of the annuity to the plaintiff's estate, and taking care of dependants.   It is difficult to fit this into a compensatory or needs-based model.   There is no guarantee that the payments will go to dependants or even to the plaintiff's family upon the death, and even looked at as a deferred instalment of a lump sum it is odd, because the loss has ceased. This characteristic demonstrates the hybrid nature of the structured settlement and to a degree reflects the de facto development of the phenomenon.

[2]   In fact, awards can be quite adequately structured without recourse to an annuity, so long as the defendant is prepared and able to meet payments indefinitely into the predicted future of the plaintiff.   However, the tax situation, which we outline at paras. 3.9 to 3.13 below, renders this an unattractive option in most cases.   Following the introduction of Crown Indemnity, Health Authorities are currently considering self-funded structures, and to date, have reached agreement on one.   We discuss this in detail at paras. 3.65 and 3.66 below.

emphasis on the maximum potential size of the awards rather than the limits suggested by life expectancies.[3]

The United States

3.2   Structured settlements were pioneered in the United States twenty five years ago to settle catastrophic injury cases, but were later used with increasing frequency by casualty insurers as a cost-savings device.[4] Their popularity led the Conference of Commissioners on Uniform State Laws to draft a model Periodic Payments of Judgments Act in 1980, hereafter referred to as the Model Act. At that time approximately fourteen states had adopted some type of statute either permitting or requiring that certain tort awards for future damages be paid in instalments. Most of the statutes were limited to medical malpractice and product liability claims. Although the Model Act was influential in improving the general design and language of subsequent periodic-payment statutes, only South Dakota adopted the Act, and then only for medical malpractice suits. It was said that the Model Act was ahead of its time and too large a step to take all at once.

3.3   The Act was revised and simplified in 1990. It now provides that any party to an action involving a claim for future damages for economic loss may elect that the Act apply. Election can be defeated by the claimant stipulating that the claim does not exceed US$100,000, or if good cause, as defined in the statute, is shown. The trier of fact is to adjust the award for inflation by including inflation as part of the damage suffered or by finding the annual rate of inflation after which the court may perform the calculations. Medical expenses and other economic losses are to be paid in the year they accrue. Defendants must secure payments by bond or annuity issued by qualified insurers designated by the Commissioner of

---

[3]   A spot survey of newspaper reports reporting on damages awards involving structuring, for the period October 1991 to May 1992, reveals that in all but one report headlines emphasised the amount of the award by referring to the total potential figure or to the 'fact' that millions were awarded. An example is the case of six year old Rebecca Field, the first case involving a Health Authority to be structured, reported in October/November 1991. Rebecca was paralysed as a result of hospital negligence at birth. The actual compensation paid out was £1.6m, of which £1,042,413 was used to purchase annuities to provide for Rebecca for the rest of her life. However, the headlines made reference to "£100m For the Love of Rebecca" (Daily Star);"£100m payout for tragic girl" (Daily Express); "The £100m Kid" (Daily Mirror); "£100m for girl crippled during birth" (Standard); "Birth injury girl settles for £100m" (The Guardian); "£100m damages for girl paralysed by hospital blunder" (The Daily Telegraph). Rebecca would have to live to old age to receive the £100m specified but her actual life expectancy was that she would live into her 30s. None of the reports mentions this, although they do refer to 'doctor's gloomy predictions'.

[4]   See Edwin G Upenieks   "Structured Settlements: Are They Here To Stay?", (1982) 3(4) Advocates Quarterly 393, at pp. 397-398. This article identifies Europe as the ultimate source, where, 30 years ago, some countries, including Sweden and Germany, initiated the use of annuities in the settlement of personal injury cases.

Insurance pursuant to the Act, but the court must also approve the funding plan overall. Plaintiffs can assign their payments but only to secure medical or other health care, spouse and child maintenance and legal fees.

3.4   By the time the 1990 version of the Model Act was promulgated, over thirty states had adopted some type of periodic-payment legislation. Originally most of the statutes were limited to cases involving medical malpractice and product liability claims, but the more recent legislation encompasses much broader areas of tort law. In addition, the United States Internal Revenue Code was amended to accommodate a system of discharging claims for bodily injury in periodic payments so that favourable tax treatment was extended beyond structured settlements. It is too soon to judge the effect of the new Model Act or to see if it will be wholly adopted by any states. Its main weakness appears to be the attempt to deal with inflation by having the trier of fact make adjustments to the award. The use of a complex formula in the 1980 version of the Model Act was thought to be one of the main reasons for that version not being adopted. The 1990 approach is a compromise which envisages juries filling out special verdict forms which appear to be quite complex in themselves.[5]

Canada

3.5   Structured settlements began to appear in Canada in 1980 in much the same form as in the United States. However, the focus is seen to be non-adversarial and is not defence-driven. [6] In Ontario section 129 of the Courts of Justice Act 1984[7] provided that, in proceedings in which damages are claimed for personal injuries or certain family law

---

[5]   See Uniform Periodic Payment of Judgments Act (1980) 14 U.L.A., for the provisions of both the 1980 and 1990 versions of the Model Act, together with commentary. Model Special Verdict Forms are set out at p. 15 of the 1990 amendment. Question 3, under 'Future Medical Expenses', asks: "[W]hat damages, if any, do you find plaintiff will sustain in the future for medical, hospital, attendant, and rehabilitative care, services, and supplies, and related expenses, as a proximate result of defendant's conduct? Include an allowance for inflation, if any, in the annual amounts for those damages, and write in the annual amounts below:

Year	Amount
19.....	$.......
19.....	$.......
19.....	$.......
19.....	$.......
19.....	$....... ..."

[6]   Structured Settlements Manual produced by McKellar Structured Settlements Inc., Ontario, Canada, 1990, at A3, note 3.

[7]   S.O. 1984, c.11.

proceedings, where all the affected parties consent, the court may order the defendant to pay all or part of the award of damages periodically. That provision was amended in 1989[8] to make such awards mandatory where the plaintiff requests that damages include an amount to compensate for income tax payable on the award unless the parties agree that such an order should not be made or the court determines that such an order would not be in the best interests of the plaintiff. The fact that the court's jurisdiction to make such an order is triggered by the plaintiff requesting that damages be grossed-up to adjust for certain inequities which arise out of the taxation of awards in Canada has been described as "an interesting Hobson's choice".[9]

3.6   In 1987 the Manitoba Law Reform Commission recommended the establishment of an optional system of non-reviewable periodic payments for any or all heads of damage.[10] The award would be at the discretion of the court and the defendant would have to provide good security. Payments would be indexed to a specified long term inflation rate. There would be a limited right for plaintiffs to assign payments. This Report has not been implemented.

3.7   In British Columbia, Structured Compensation Bills were introduced in 1989 and 1990. Although the latter bill was referred to a standing committee, before the committee reported there was a change of government. The Structured Compensation Bill 1990 allows the court to make a structured compensation order if the defendant is backed by an insurer. The court can require the defendant's insurer to purchase a single premium annuity contract which must be non-assignable, non-commutable and non-transferable. The court can override the wishes of the plaintiff regarding future loss and order periodic payments where it considers this is in the best interests of the parties.[11]

3.8   The absence of any sort of periodic payment scheme was lamented throughout the 1980s by the courts in Canada in cases where judges felt a lump sum payment was inappropriate.[12] In 1987, courts, in both Manitoba and British Columbia asserted an inherent jurisdiction to award compensation in the form of periodic payments. However, the Supreme

---

[8]   By S.O. 1989, c.67. The current provision is now contained in s. 116 of the Courts of Justice Act, R.S.O. 1990, chap. C.43.

[9]   Letter from the Chairman, Law Reform Commission of British Columbia, 30 April 1992.

[10]   *Manitoba Report No. 68*, pp. 63 and 77.

[11]   Letter from Chairman, Law Reform Commission of British Columbia, 30 April 1992.

[12]   For example, *Lewis* v. *Todd and McClure* [1980] 2 S.C.R. 694, 710; *MacDonald* v. *Alderson and Manitoba* [1982] 3 W.W.R. 385, 389, 390 and 395; *McErlean* v. *Sarel* [1987] 61 O.R. (2d) 396, 433.

Court of Canada, in *Watkins* v. *Olafson*[13] held that, in the absence of legislation, the courts have no power to award the periodic payment of damages. It is apparent that in Canada the position regarding the periodic payment of damages is very much in a state of transition.

England and Wales

3.9   Structured settlements are now established in the United Kingdom to the extent that it is regularly suggested that solicitors dealing with personal injury cases have a professional duty to consider structuring in appropriate cases.[14] A 1987 decision by the Revenue was the genesis for the development of structuring in this country. Although lump sum payments are themselves not subject to tax, any interest earned from subsequent investment is. Periodic payments were also regarded as taxable in the hands of the plaintiff. Thus, there was no perceived tax advantage in structuring an award rather than investing a lump sum. However, in 1978-79 in the United States, and in 1980 in Canada, the revenue authorities conceded tax-free status to structured settlements. This process considerably boosted the use of such settlements in North America. It was mirrored in the United Kingdom by an agreement reached between the Inland Revenue and the Association of British Insurers (ABI) in mid-1987.[15]

3.10   The Revenue considered that the 1936 case of *Dott* v. *Brown*[16] allowed payments to a plaintiff arising from an annuity arranged by the defendants to be treated as capital and not income[17]. Payments arising from such settlements therefore have a tax-free status. The Revenue approved four model agreements, drafted by and agreed between it and the ABI. The agreements were intended to cover the four main kinds of periodic payment likely to be required. A *Basic Terms* agreement allows pre-set

---

[13]   [1989] 2 S.C.R. 750, (1989) 61 D.L.R. (4th) 577.

[14]   See, for example, Gail Rifkind, "The Nuts and Bolts of Structured Settlements", (1992) The Lawyer, 6. Rifkind also states that structured settlements look set to replace the conventional lump sum.

[15]   Whilst the agreement applies to all of the United Kingdom, our analysis of the underlying law concerning personal injury damages and provisional recommendations for reform relate only to England and Wales.

[16]   [1936] 1 All E.R. 543 (C.A.).

[17]   For a discussion of whether the Revenue's interpretation of *Dott* is correct, see C. Francis, "Taxation of Structured Settlements", Notes of Cases, [1991] British Tax Review, 56. Francis argues that the view that annual payments are capital, not income, may be wrong where payments are RPI linked. However, she concludes that it is likely taxpayers can rely on the letter from the Revenue giving its view of the plaintiff's future tax liability, because no other taxpayer has locus standi to challenge the decision. We do not propose to pursue this aspect further since our enquiries have not revealed any serious challenge to the Revenue's interpretation of *Dott*.

payments to run for a fixed period. An *Indexed Terms* agreement links the payments in a Basic Terms agreement to the Retail Price Index to make them inflation-proof. A *Terms for Life* agreement allows pre-set payments to continue until the plaintiff's death, and there may be a pre-set minimum number of payments. *Indexed Terms for Life* are inflation-proof Terms for Life. The Revenue has essentially given such agreements advance clearance provided they are in the standard form. The four forms are not necessarily the only ones acceptable to the Revenue but variations require individual clearance.

3.11 Because structured settlements are still in their infancy, it appears common practice to obtain individual clearance. In *Kelly* v. *Dawes* [18] Potter J. suggested that confirmation by the Revenue that a proposed settlement was within the agreed guidelines would be appropriate in any case where a court was being asked to approve a structured settlement. This has been confirmed in a Practice Note.[19] With the increasing use of this form of settlement, especially out of court, the Inland Revenue may encourage full use of the model agreement procedure so as to obviate the need for individual clearance. This should happen in any event as the profession gains confidence and experience with the structuring of damages.

3.12 The agreement between the ABI and the Revenue assumes that the defendant's insurer will wish to reinsure its liability by purchasing a life annuity from a life insurer. In a typical case, the defendant's insurer agrees to pay damages by instalments which last for the life of the plaintiff and are index-linked. The annuity from the life office runs back-to-back with this agreement and funds those payments. The life office has to deduct tax from the payments it makes to the defendant's insurer pursuant to the life policy. Because its contract is with the defendant's insurer, the life office cannot make payments direct to the plaintiff. There must be discontinuity between the annuity contract and the structured settlement, otherwise the character of the payments to the plaintiff change - they would become income and subject to tax.

3.13 The defendant's insurer remains separately liable to the plaintiff, and must gross-up the payments it makes to the plaintiff to cover the deduction previously made by the life office. The defendant's insurer is later able to recover the cost of grossing up as a deduction from profits for corporation tax, or by claiming repayment from the Revenue. But pending this it must carry this cost. It also bears the costs of administering the scheme. This situation differs from North America where annuities which relate to personal injury or fatal accident cases can be paid directly by the life office as agent of the insurer to the plaintiff without deduction

---

[18]   *The Times*, 27 September 1990; *Kemp & Kemp*, vol. 1, 6A - 110.

[19]   (Structured Settlements : Court's Approval)[1992] 1 W.L.R. 328 (H.Ct).

of tax, provided the annuity is non-transferable, non-commutable and non-assignable.[20]   The reason structured settlements are attractive to insurance companies in the United Kingdom in spite of these drawbacks is that they are able to negotiate with the plaintiff for a discount from the sum to be invested in the annuity. The discounts reflect uncertainties in the claim as well as the fact that the income from the annuities will not be taxable in the hands of the plaintiff. The structured settlement package, the discount, and the annuity are usually established by agreement between the parties, with the assistance of intermediaries who may have forensic accounting expertise and knowledge of the life markets.[21]

The Advantages of Structured Settlements

3.14   One of the advantages of structuring is said to be that it benefits both parties, thereby encouraging early settlement with attendant savings in cost and time. Parties that are far apart on a lump sum figure are able to take a different approach which may eventually lead to an acceptable compromise.

3.15   The main advantage cited for plaintiffs is certainty. This consists of a number of elements. The plaintiff is relieved of the burden of managing a large sum of money and is protected from possible dissipation of the funds. She or he is assured of regular payments for life and of payments to dependants if there is a longer guarantee period, and is also assured the payments will not decline in value if they are index-linked.[22] These features make structured settlements particularly apt where there are serious injuries and the conventional award would be large, and especially where the plaintiff is a child and a long period of future care is envisaged. It is regarded as unlikely the state will ever have to step in to provide for the plaintiff where a settlement is structured.

---

[20]   Revenue Canada Taxation Bulletin No. IT-365R2, 8 May 1987, s. 5. Non-assignability now only relates to the plaintiff. Revenue Canada has agreed that the defendant insurer can conditionally assign its obligations and liabilities prior to purchase of an annuity to an eligible assignee with the plaintiff's written agreement. This is intended to remove perceived difficulties in structuring faced by self-insurers, non-resident foreign insurers and reinsurers, and insolvent insurers. See Robert G. Watkin, "The New Method of Structuring Settlement Agreements",Can. B.R., (1992), vol. 71, 27.

[21]   Frenkel Topping Structured Settlements, a subsidiary of a firm of accountants, has acted in an intermediary capacity in a very substantial majority of structured settlements in the United Kingdom of which we are aware.   Other intermediaries are Touche Ross and Co., The Structured Settlements Company, Ltd (which acts only for insurers and self-insurance defendants), Godwins Structured Settlements, and Structured Compensation (a subsidiary of Hogg Robinson & Gardner Mountain plc, the Lloyds insurance brokers). Many accountancy firms offer specialised advice on structuring as part of their general practice.

[22]   Richard Lewis, "Pensions Replace Lump Sum Damages",(1988) 15 J. Law. Soc 392, at p. 403.

3.16   Flexibility is seen as a further attractive feature of structuring for the plaintiff. The projected settlement can be individually tailored to the plaintiff's needs. Damages are linked to life expectancy without an absolute date having to be specified to provide a cut-off point. Annual income is also based on projected future cash requirements. Provided these are considered carefully, the annuity package can be set up to provide at the appropriate time for education, changing nursing needs, asset accumulation, housing, marriage and children, and limited work or business prospects, if any. The damages will not be spent before these needs arise. The key is the inclusion of periodic lump sums at key stages in the plaintiff's life.[23] Thus, structuring focuses on the plaintiff's needs, unlike the conventionally assessed lump sum, thereby in principle reducing the adversarial nature of the proceedings.

3.17   It must be said that it is not exactly clear how the focus of negotiation has shifted. The Model Agreements provide for the recording of an overall sum (intended to be calculated in the conventional manner) which is then to be broken down into the structure. However, our investigations have led us to conclude that there is no consistent approach to the starting point for structured settlements. It is said that the proper approach is for the defendant to make an offer to settle on a conventional basis which should then lead to discussions about structuring. The claim should always be valued first in the ordinary way.[24] However, there have been reports of cases where the reverse has occurred and the parties simply structured the amount the plaintiff needed.[25] Further, it is difficult to see that a conventional lump sum has ever been agreed in a case where the plaintiffs claimed £1.1 million and the defendants offered £600,0000, whence both parties moved straight in to structuring what emerged as a completely different figure.[26] This development has interesting practical and philosophical implications which are discussed at paragraphs 3.57 to 3.60 below.

3.18   Finally, the tax advantages of structured settlements, which have already been outlined,[27] have been the real catalyst for the development of this form of award for both plaintiff and defendant. Tax savings to the plaintiff could currently be a maximum of 40%. The plaintiff is

---

[23]   See materials for Structured Settlements Seminar, 3 December 1991, prepared by John Frenkel of Frenkel Topping Structured Settlements (hereafter *Frenkel Topping Materials*), pp. 10-11.

[24]   Guy Mansfield, "Structured settlements - an introduction", (1991) 135(47) S.J. 1317 .

[25]   See Fiona Bawdon, "A System Where Both Sides Win?", (1992) 6(6) The Lawyer, 5.

[26]   *Braybrooke* v. *Parker* (Unreported), 22 October 1991, H.Ct, No.90NJ 3965. Case referred to at an Action for Victims of Medical Accidents Lawyers Support Group Meeting held 3 December 1991, London (hereafter 'AVMA Lawyers Support Group Meeting').

[27]   Above, paras. 3.9-3.13.

immunized against future increases in personal tax rates. The tax saving is also a negotiating tool, since it can fund any discount requested by the defendant. We examine and ask questions about the nature of the discount and the defendant's 'right' to share in the plaintiff's tax savings at paragraphs 3.28 to 3.30 below.

The Disadvantages of Structured Settlements

3.19   Structured settlements do not avoid the need for forecasting. In fact they may place an undesirable emphasis on this aspect which is avoided where lump sums are used. Whereas with the latter the plaintiff has to deal with anticipated future needs by managing the lump sum and making payments to meet the needs as required, a structured settlement requires experts and advisors to prepare a complex advance budget for life. Once determined, structured settlements cannot be changed - they only have initial flexibility.[28] Therefore, the pressure to 'get it right' at that initial stage is extreme. Payments from annuities may come on stream at the wrong time or not be needed at all. Prognoses may yet prove to be incorrect, affecting decisions previously made about lifestyle. The problem is ameliorated to a degree by building a contingency fund into the structure, but obvious advice noting that this fund should be 'appropriate' or 'substantial' is of limited guidance.[29] Overall, however, we consider that structured settlements do improve matters in relation to the uncertainty inherent in making provision for the future. Structured settlements, in contrast to lump sum awards, can take better account of economic factors and life expectancy. The uncertainties which remain are not currently capable of being resolved without making structured settlements reviewable. This question is addressed at paragraphs 3.39-3.46, 3.85, 3.90, and 5.21.

3.20   Structured settlements also do not completely remove the risk that the monies thereby provided will not in fact be adequate to meet the plaintiff's needs. In fact the plaintiff, unless subject to supervision by the Court of Protection, is still able to squander any monies she or he receives even if intended for specific purposes. But it should be noted that with regard to the latter at least, the plaintiff is in no different position from the ordinary wage or salary earner. Control of income use in this context would seem unacceptable. Another aspect of the risk is that although structures are

---

[28]   *Frenkel Topping Materials,* p. 11, para. 5.

[29]   McKellar Structured Settlements Inc., Ontario, Canada, has implemented thousands of structures over the last thirteen years, keeping a file for every such structure. There are few complaints, and only approximately three complaints about insufficient money. This is because with the structured settlement printout in front of the claimant, she or he plans to live within that budget. However, it is also possible that where funds are not sufficient, claimants realise there is no point in complaining to the company. (Letter from Frank McKellar to the Commission dated 27 May 1992).

linked to the RPI via the index-linked annuity, this cannot guarantee that costs of future care will always be met. Historically, the cost of care has always moved ahead of the RPI. To this extent, the shortfall has to be made up from the contingency fund. Structures are by no means perfect.

3.21 Finally, a structured settlement, although apparently benefiting a plaintiff in all ways, may simply be undesired by the individual plaintiff. For example, a severely injured plaintiff may wish to take a large lump sum in order to move to another country to take advantage of educational or business opportunities there.[30]his raises the question of whether the courts should be given the power to impose structured settlements against the parties' wills, and if so, on what grounds.

Proposals for Reform of Structured Settlements

Introduction

3.22 We believe that the availability of structured settlements as a remedy in personal injury cases in the United Kingdom should not now be seriously questioned. Though it has been said that their development has been somewhat 'in the shadow of the law',[31] we believe that the advantages clearly outweigh any disadvantages, and that the availability of structuring is a useful option which can benefit plaintiffs, particularly given the high incidence of cases that are settled. However, because of their genesis within the existing tax framework, fine distinctions have to be made to achieve structured settlements. They also involve administrative arrangements which some regard as cumbersome. We therefore turn to consider proposals for reform. These fall into two categories. The first is broadly concerned to address the existing voluntary regime and to rationalise it while preserving its voluntary nature. The second is concerned with proposals for more fundamental reform empowering the court to impose a structured settlement. We deal with the rationalising proposals first at paragraphs 3.23 - 3.70 below because, subject to the views of consultees, we consider that, whether or not the more major proposals for change are accepted, the existing regime should be rationalised. But it is the major proposals involving the supplementation of the existing voluntary regime by the creation of a power in the court to order a structured settlement, which undoubtedly raise substantial issues

---

[30] An actual case encountered by Frenkel Topping. Interview with Ivor Levy, 9 December 1991.

[31] Richard Lewis "Pensions Replace Lump Sum Damages",(1988) 15 J. Law. Soc.392, at p. 394; Lewis, "Structured Settlements", (1988) vol.138 N. L. J. 660, at p. 667. The decision of the Inland Revenue has been described as ad hoc and made in the absence of any coherent policy for compensating the disabled. Structured settlements have been said to benefit a group already receiving the highest benefits. The scope of our review prevents us from exploring this aspect of structuring further.

of principle and practice in the law of damages. These are considered at paragraphs 3.71 - 3.98 below.

Proposals for rationalisation of the existing voluntary regime

(a) Introduction

3.23   These proposals fall into three categories. The first comprises issues arising out of the possibility of rationalising the current tax arrangements so as to provide similarity of treatment as between different kinds of defendant (or rather their insurers) and the question of whether structured settlements should be reviewable. The second comprises issues arising out of a possible need to monitor the negotiating process, while the third covers administrative issues involved in the process of structuring and managing it thereafter. It is then necessary to revisit the matter of actuarial evidence considered above in Part II.

(b) Rationalisation of the tax regime

(i) Additional expense to the defendant's insurer

3.24   As mentioned in paragraph 3.13 above, structuring under the present tax regime causes expense to the defendant's insurer in two respects which is avoided under the tax regime for structured settlements in North America. First, the insurer suffers a loss in cash flow as it can only recover at the end of each year the difference between the net sums which it receives from the life office and the gross sums which it pays the plaintiff. Thus, there is a consequent cash flow interruption for the insurer. Second, an additional administrative burden is placed on the insurer. However, the Revenue has informed us that it is not possible to retain the favourable tax status of periodic payments made under an approved structured settlement if the life office pays the plaintiff directly. For these to be treated as instalments of a capital sum and therefore untaxable, they have to arise under the settlement with the insurer which establishes an antecedent debt. The insurer stands in the shoes of the defendant and becomes liable. That liability cannot be transferred except by novation or, conceivably, under the provisions of sections 51 and 52 of the Insurance Companies Act 1982[32]. The essential discontinuity between the annuity contract and the structured settlement would be broken if liability was assumed by the life office. Further, the Revenue believes novation would almost certainly alter the character of the payments with the result that they would fall to be treated as income in the hands of the plaintiff[33] and therefore taxable.

---

[32]   Transfers of general business by insurance companies to other bodies, with the approval of the Secretary of State.

[33]   Letter to Law Commission dated 13 January 1992.

3.25   We invite comment on whether the situation outlined in paragraph 3.24 above does indeed act as a significant disincentive to this form of settlement. Our provisional view is that the problem may be overstated. The cost of the loss of cashflow and administration will no doubt be allowed for by the defendant's insurer in negotiating the discount. Administrative costs should be minimal in any event - computerisation facilitates the standardisation of the necessary systems which will also be used for other profit-making purposes.

3.26   However, a further question of principle arises. It seems to us that structuring confers a benefit on the state in that it is less likely that a plaintiff who receives a structured settlement will later become dependant on the state. The Revenue has recognised the economic and social advantages of structuring.[34] Accordingly, we think it is inequitable that, as between the defendant or the defendant's insurer and the tax authorities, the former should have to bear the cost of the loss of cash flow and of administration, even though the costs may be passed on in the long run. We invite comment on this proposition.

3.27   If the disincentive is real, or if the view we express in paragraph 3.26 above is compelling, we believe the answer would be to make legislative provision allowing the life insurer to take over the obligation of making the payments and the defendant's insurer to close the file. It is not necessary for actual liability to be assumed by the life office. In Canada the owner of the annuity, traditionally the insurer, must guarantee the payments in the event of the default of the life office. This is deemed a notional liability because none of the life offices has defaulted on payments. Thus, the fiscal neutrality of the arrangement is maintained. We also invite comment on this proposal.

3.28   The insurer will often try to take full account of the entire cost of a structured settlement by seeking a discount on the settlement figure. The size of the discount ranges from 8% to 15%, with an average of around 10%[35]. It may be helpful to give some examples by way of illustration. In all cases we assume that the plaintiff buys her or his own annuity. We begin with the position of the plaintiff who is not liable to any tax at all. Ignoring mortality considerations and following the court's practice of assuming a 4.5% reduction in the multiplier, the appropriate multiplier for a plaintiff expecting a loss stretching over 20 years can be read off from Net Present Value tables[36] as approximately 13. Assuming the plaintiff's

---

[34]   In an article by the Senior Principal Inspector, Insurance and Specialist Division, Inland Revenue - M. Newstead, "Tax aspects of structured settlements", (1989) 7(10) The Litigation Letter 78.

[35]   "Structured Settlements - A Practitioner's Viewpoint", a paper prepared for the Commission by Frenkel Topping Structured Settlements, May 1992, p. 7.

[36]   For example, those in Higson, *Business Finance* (1986).

annual loss is £5,000, the lump sum in this case would be just over £65,000. Secondly, we consider the position of a person who is liable to tax. In such cases the Inland Revenue will take its normal approach of charging tax on the income element of annuity proceeds. On the assumption that this is one of the exceptional situations in which courts make allowance for tax,[37] the corresponding multiplier will depend on the rate of tax. At the standard rate of 25% it will be approximately 14.25 and at the higher rate of 40% it will be just over 15. The lump sums in question, again assuming an annual loss of £5,000, will be £71,250 and about £75,000 respectively. These multipliers, in particular that of approximately 13 which would apply in all but exceptional cases, would thus be relevant to a defendant who is contemplating a structured settlement with a plaintiff, for the purposes of considering an appropriate discount.

3.29   For a standard rate taxpayer the total value of the tax payments due on the plaintiff-bought annuity amounts to only a little over 8% of the value of the annuity. This percentage figure represents the bottom line of the percentage figures typically charged by defendants to enter into structures. In such a case the insurer is diverting all that is saved in tax to reduce the cost to it of the award and there would be no financial incentive for the plaintiff to agree to a structure as she or he would be no better off. This may account for some of the 50% of all major settlements which do not structure. It might be thought that an insurer who wishes to structure would be content with a discount slightly smaller than the net present value of the tax saving to the plaintiff. However, since discounts are averaging 10%, it is apparent that plaintiffs accepting structures in such cases take account of other incentives, such as the strength of the case, the desire to settle it and the desire to achieve certainty of future payments.

3.30   We are interested to know what elements go into the determination of the discount. Does it reflect for the insurer the additional costs of a structured settlement (as against the lump sum which must otherwise be paid) or something else? Why do plaintiffs accept discounts greater than the tax saving? If the discount is purely to cover administration and other costs, their removal would logically remove the need for a discount. If, however, the discount includes some element recognising the legitimacy of the insurer in participating in the tax benefits, removal of administrative difficulties would not make it altogether illegitimate for the insurer to seek a discount. How large should such an element be? Unless the view is taken that the defendant is entitled to more than the costs of entering into the settlement because this facilitates out of court compromises and provides the plaintiff with certainty, the removal of one disincentive in this context could be seen as creating another. We seek comment on this aspect.

---

[37]   In *Hodgson* v. *Trapp* [1989] A.C. 807, these were said to be exceptional. See para 2.40 above.

(ii) Non-corporation tax payers

3.31 The second disincentive seen as arising from the tax position in the United Kingdom also derives from the deduction of tax by the life office. Because the defendant's insurer can only recover the amount of gross-up on the payments it makes to the plaintiff by setting it off against its corporation tax, non-corporation tax payers have no opportunity to claim back such sums at all. Mutual insurance companies are not trading insurers and are not subject to corporation tax. They can therefore only structure with a tax loss. The medical defence unions are in the same position. Area Health Authorities were in the same position as they are exempt from paying corporation tax. However, the Revenue has now advised that they can claim repayment of income tax deducted from the annuity payments. This decision of the Revenue is important as large awards of damages for future loss are often claimed in medical negligence actions. Again, the Revenue's response to the suggestion that mutual insurance companies, the medical defence unions and public bodies other than Area Health Authorities suffer a tax disincentive to structure, emphasises that no new tax advantages have been created. Income tax is deducted from the annuity by the life office as required by statute, but is available for set-off against the insurer's corporation tax liability. The tax treatment is the same as it would be if the general insurer made some other investment to fund its liabilities. The Revenue suggests that the only non-corporation taxpayers likely to be involved, apart from Lloyds syndicates, are Health Authorities, with regard to which the Revenue notes its recent advice allowing the tax to be reclaimed.[38]

3.32 We again invite comment on the extent to which this situation is in practice a disincentive to structure. We note that the problem of mutuality can be circumvented in certain types of case, so as to obtain the full tax benefits a normal trading insurer is able to achieve.[39] However, it is our provisional view that, if the problem with regard to mutual insurers and public bodies other than Area Health Authorities is significant, it would seem equitable for the Revenue to allow tax to be reclaimed in appropriately specified instances as it has done for Health Authorities. The alternative and more far-reaching solution is that outlined in paragraph 3.27 above, of allowing the life office to pay instalments of damages direct to the plaintiff, thus cutting out altogether the need for the insurer to gross up payments and claim back tax at a later stage.

3.33 Our provisional view is to favour the latter solution which has the virtue of eliminating a number of problems. In order for the plaintiff to receive the payments due in full, this solution would have to go hand in hand with

---

[38] Letter to Law Commission dated 13 January 1992.

[39] *Kemp & Kemp*, vol. 1, 6A-078 - 6A-079.

an extension of the tax status currently given to settlements which conform to the Model Agreements. The same tax status would have to be accorded to all annuities purchased by defendants or defendants' insurers in actions for personal injury or under the Fatal Accidents Acts. This would require a careful legislative definition of 'personal injury'. We invite comment on this proposition. We do not go further and recommend that the tax reform outlined above be extended to annuities purchased with any sort of damages award. Preferential treatment for the victims of personal injury is justified to a degree because there is a strong public interest in specific needs, that would otherwise necessarily be met by the welfare system or public institutions such as the NHS, being met out of the award over a long period of time. Victims of defamation, conversion or breach of contract are less likely to become dependent on the state because of the wrong done to them and are less likely to have continuing long term future needs.

(iii) CICB and MIB

3.34 At present, there is debate about whether payments made by the Criminal Injuries Compensation Board (CICB) and the Motor Insurers Bureau (MIB) may be the subject of a structured settlement. It is not clear whether the CICB is able to purchase annuities and administer structured settlements because of the status of the Board itself. The Board was set up under the prerogative but legislation (not yet in force) has been passed to put it on a purely statutory basis.[40] The payments it makes under the scheme it administers are "ex gratia" and therefore do not comply with the requirement there must exist an antecedent debt for annuity payments to be treated as payments of capital and not subject to tax. The ex gratia nature of payments is in reality a fiction since the Board is instructed and compelled to make payments to all who satisfy the requirements of the scheme, refusal to do so being susceptible by an application for judicial review.

3.35 In cases where the defendant is an uninsured driver the MIB has agreed[41] to pay damages due to the plaintiff if judgment is not satisfied in full by

---

[40] Sections 108-117 of the Criminal Justice Act 1988 establish the scheme, but under s. 171(1) come into effect on a day yet to be appointed. There are no current plans to implement the relevant provisions. The revised 1990 scheme (*Hansard* (H.L.), 8 December 1989, vol. 163, cols. 410-417 (Written Answers), copies also available from the Board), came into force on 1 February 1990. Consideration is being given to the question whether it would be practical or appropriate to introduce the concept of structured settlements for CICS awards. (Letter from the Home Office to Law Commission, 14 July 1992).

[41] By agreement concluded on 22 November 1972 between it and the Secretary of State for the Environment. Copies are available from HMSO. The text of the agreement is set out in J. Pritchard, *Personal Injury Litigation* (6th ed., 1989), Appendix H, p. 286.

the judgment debtor within seven days.[42] There are three categories of action - the untraced driver (a hit-and-run), the uninsured driver (the defendant has no insurance and no means), and the domestic agreement case (the defendant was driving outside the terms of her or his insurance policy). In the first case payments are effectively ex gratia. In the second, uncertainty about the Board's tax status is currently preventing structuring. In the third, we understand that the Inland Revenue has advised that structuring is possible.[43] Both the CICB and the MIB are also reluctant to take on the administrative difficulties involved in passing on payments from the life offices to the plaintiff.

3.36   We are of the provisional view that both these boards should be able to structure. It is inequitable that a particular class of plaintiff is unable to structure simply because she or he has the misfortune of being injured by a criminal or a defendant who is not insured. Our reasons are similar to those concerning non trading and other insurers at paragraph 3.33 above. Provided the solution proposed in paragraph 3.33 is adopted, and MIB and CICB are then able to enter into structured settlements in the form of a suitable Model Agreement, in our provisional view the tax advantages should be available. We note, however, that the Criminal Injuries Compensation Scheme might require amendment. Paragraph 12 of the 1990 revised scheme provides that compensation is normally to take the form of a lump sum. However, this is subject to paragraph 9, which grants a general discretion to the Board to make special arrangements for the administration of an award. This provision, combined with the fact that applicants do not have a 'right' to compensation under the scheme, and that decisions of the Board are final, with no right to appeal,[44] means that were the CICB in a position to structure an award made by it, it would have the power to impose such an award against the wishes of the plaintiff. The answers of consultees to the questions we pose at paragraphs 3.74 to 3.89 will determine whether such a position would be desirable. We invite comment on this general solution to the difficulties with the tax regime outlined above.

(iv) Court-ordered structures

3.37   The fourth concern relevant to rationalisation of the tax regime arises from the fact that at present, structures ordered by a court with the consent of both parties do not attract the tax benefits. In *Burke v. Tower Hamlets*

---

[42]   On the operation and general administration of the MIB, see *MacGillivray and Parkington on Insurance Law* (8th ed., 1988), paras. 2086-2104; *Colinvaux's Law of Insurance* (6th ed., 1990), paras. 20-33 to 20-61, pp. 350-362.

[43]   Advice from Frenkel Topping Structured Settlements, June 1992.

[44]   Judicial review is possible (*R. v. C.I.C.B., ex p. Lain* [1967] 2 Q.B. 864).

Health Authority,[45]   Drake J. held that periodic payment of damages could not be ordered except by consent. Therefore, at least where the parties consent, a court can in theory order a structure. However, since a court order would currently wipe out any tax advantage to the plaintiff, no judge is likely to be asked to make such an order.[46] We also discuss this problem in relation to provisional damages[47]. We have been made aware of some concern that because structuring is still a new concept there is a risk that parties may allow a lump sum to be awarded by a court and then decide it would be a good idea to structure. To avoid this problem, and to ensure consistency, it is our provisional view that Model Agreements incorporated into a consent order should have the tax advantage.   Hence, there would be a point in parties seeking such a remedy, or indeed, in the court suggesting that the parties consider structuring.   We invite comment on this proposition.

3.38   The question remains whether legislation is also required to confirm that, where the parties consent, a court is empowered to order structures with consent.   Although it is possible that the Court of Appeal or House of Lords will in the future overturn the decision in *Burke*[48], and judicially create a major new power with regard to damages, this is unlikely. Therefore, subject to the views of consultees, we think that for reasons of certainty it would be desirable to clarify the situation by making legislative provision for judicial power to order a structure where both parties consent.

(v) Reviewability

3.39   In paragraph 3.19 we commented both on the initial flexibility of structured settlements and on the fact that once entered into they cannot be changed. Parties entering into a structured settlement will usually seek to provide for unanticipated needs resulting from the injury to the plaintiff, such as when the plaintiff's condition deteriorates and further expenditure is necessitated, by means of a contingency fund. The first question that arises is whether the provision of such a fund is seen as adequate to cope with the vicissitudes of life. We believe that the size of the contingency fund varies a great deal from case to case. It appears to be a residual fund, its size depending on how much is left over after the provision of

---

[45]   *The Times*, 10 August 1989.

[46]   Even where the court may be involved in simply approving a structure, it cannot make any order in the proceedings. The Model Agreements allow only the parties to agree on the fixed sum of the debt to be structured - all legal proceedings must be discontinued. Thus, a lump sum ordered by a court cannot later be structured without then becoming liable to tax as income.

[47]   See para. 5.21 below.

[48]   *The Times*, 10 August 1989.

annuities. It can be reduced by operation of the new provisions for recoupment of DSS benefits, which are discussed at paragraph 4.5 below. We have heard of cases where no contingency fund at all was provided. We invite comment on the adequacy of the contingency fund as a means of meeting needs not provided for by other benefits in the structured settlement.

3.40 If the contingency fund is not seen as adequate, the question arises whether structured settlements should be reviewable. Reviewability could take either of two forms. One would be that new money, additional to that put into the original settlement, would be provided. The other would be that the unexpended benefits from the original settlement would be restructured in a way that better met the needs of the plaintiff.

3.41 The possibility of reviewability to provide new money for plaintiffs has received previous consideration both by this Commission and the Pearson Commission. In 1971 the Law Commission considered the possibility that damages be awarded in the form of variable periodic payments which the court either was obliged or had a discretion to order instead of the conventional lump sum.[49] Variability was seen as essential to ameliorate the injustice caused by inaccurate forecasting.[50] No other system was considered. We expressed our support for upwards-only reviews, because if awards could be reviewed downwards plaintiffs would be encouraged to malinger with the attendant possibility of secret surveillance of the plaintiff by insurance companies.[51] We also expressed a strong preference for a discretionary rather than an obligatory system but reached no conclusion on whether such a system ought to be introduced.[52] The suggestion of variable periodic payments met with strong disapproval on consultation and was not recommended in the final report,[53] but the objections were directed more at the notion of periodic payments simpliciter, rather than reviewability as a particular feature. Five years later, on receiving substantial evidence in favour of periodic payments, the Pearson Commission recommended the introduction of a pension system as a remedy available to the court in cases of serious injury or death.[54] The pension was to be reviewable by the court to the extent of taking account of inflation and deterioration in the plaintiff's medical condition, provided that the latter led to financial loss. More comprehensive review

---

[49] *Personal Injury Litigation - Assessment of Damages* W.P.41, paras. 226-252.

[50] *Ibid.*, para.227.

[51] *Ibid.*, paras. 243-4.

[52] *Ibid.*, para.240.

[53] (1973) Law Com. No.56 (1973), paras. 26-30.

[54] The *Pearson Report*, vol.1, pp.122-5, paras. 555-573.

was seen as too complicated, at least initially. Like the Law Commission, the Pearson Commission saw reviewability as essential to achieve the advantage that periodic payments could take account of actual changes following trial. These recommendations of the Pearson Commission were not implemented.

3.42   If the contingency fund is not an adequate means of providing for unexpected needs resulting from the plaintiff's injury, the reviewability of the structured settlement in order to meet those needs is in principle desirable so as to achieve restitutio in integrum. Consistently with that purpose, in our view if there is to be reviewability, it should be triggered by any deterioration in the plaintiff's medical condition arising out of the original injury, provided that it has caused further financial loss. However for the reasons given in our 1971 Working Paper[55] we do not think that an improvement in the plaintiff's condition should enable a review to take place. We also do not believe that the effect of inflation should make structures reviewable. Most structures are, we understand, based on annuities which are index-linked where appropriate.

3.43   In paragraph 3.90 below we consider whether the court should be able to impose restructuring on a voluntary structured settlement by allowing one or both of the parties to apply to the court for review. But we now turn to the question whether steps could or should be taken to facilitate the voluntary inclusion in structured settlements of provisions for reviewability. Parties are free at present to agree reviewable structured settlements. But in practice they appear never to do so.

3.44   The primary legal obstacle to parties agreeing a structured settlement which allows for reviewability in the form of the provision of new money is that it would not appear to attract the tax benefits now afforded to annuities which repay a fixed pre-existing debt. The Model Agreements approved by the Revenue do not contemplate a reviewable debt. The tax legislation would have to be amended if periodic payments under a reviewable structure were to be tax-free in the hands of the plaintiff. But even if such amendment could be procured, we very much doubt if defendants would agree to such reviewability. The possibility of a reviewable settlement would allow the defendant to negotiate to reduce the size of the lump sum paid in addition to the amount structured since reviewability would largely remove the need for a contingency fund. It would also give the defendant the option of agreeing to defer payment of part of the award upon a contingency that may never arise. However, there are a number of disadvantages to defendants which are likely to outweigh these advantages. The defendant's insurers would not be able to close their books because of the unlimited further liability they would thereby be undertaking. It is far from clear that the life insurance industry

---

[55]   (1971) *Personal Injury Litigation - Assessment of Damages*, para. 243.

would be able or prepared to offer annuities accommodating reviewability. The exercise would be costly because insurers would have to purchase a new package of assets to back the new policies. Varying insurance contracts also involves costs because insurers recover the commission paid to intermediaries and other costs in the early days of a policy. If those costs are to be borne by defendants, they will be deterred from agreeing to reviewability. If they are to be borne by plaintiffs, this would detract from the benefit to them conferred by reviewability.

3.45 It may well be that structured settlements which provide for reviewability in the form of a restructuring of the original agreement would not have any tax disadvantages: they do not carry the implication that there is a reviewable debt. Consequently, if that be correct, no changes to the tax legislation would be needed. Reviewability in this form has the considerable merit for defendants that no new money need be provided. However, as matters now stand, parties are free to agree at any time in the life of a structure that it should be rearranged even if it is not a term of the original agreement. In principle this may be undesirable because knowledge that the structure is reviewable if predictions prove to be incorrect might encourage less care being taken at the initial stage. It might also encourage plaintiffs to seek review for reasons of mere dissatisfaction rather than need. Moreover in practice it seems to us that only in rare circumstances would it be practical to have such a review. The need for a review, we assume, would usually be caused by a new or additional need, but no new money is to be provided. Further, there would be costs in rearranging the structure and they would no doubt have to be borne by the plaintiff.

3.46 Our provisional conclusion is that amending the tax legislation is unlikely to lead to the greater use of voluntary reviewable settlements, but we would welcome comments on this. However, in paragraph 5.21 below we consider a form of reviewability in connection with awards of provisional and interim damages.

(c) The need to monitor the negotiation process

(i) The position of the intermediary

3.47 Concern has been expressed about the position of and form of payment to the intermediaries who currently provide professional accountancy advice to parties wishing to structure. We understand that often the same accountant will advise both parties whilst holding herself or himself out as independent. Where a defendant instructs an intermediary who then purports to act for both parties,[56] the curious position exists that,

---

[56] See, for example, *Beck* v. *Plasticisers Ltd (Readicut International plc)* (1992) 8(6) P. &. M.I.L.L. No 6, 41.

although the intermediary acts on the instructions of the defendant, the intermediary's costs are indirectly met by the plaintiff through payment of commission on the annuity. This raises questions of conflict of interest and to whom duties of care are owed, questions which arise in many other contexts involving intermediaries and professional advisers.

3.48 The intermediaries see themselves as simply 'cutting the cloth' supplied by the parties,[57] but it is apparent that the point at which intermediaries first become involved in negotiations and the extent of their influence on the negotiations varies considerably from case to case and must be affected by how experienced the legal representatives are in structuring. We seek the views of consultees as to what exactly is happening in practice and whether a real problem is seen to exist. The questions which arise are firstly whether intermediaries should be able to act for both parties; secondly, whether they act for one or both parties, what the extent of their duties is; thirdly, whether the fact that the plaintiff has legal advisers who should supervise the settlement is inadequate protection; and finally, whether the law of negligence provides adequate protection for the plaintiff and the defendant.

3.49 Should intermediaries be able to act for both parties? In our view the mere fact of acting for both parties may not be unacceptable where both parties, made fully aware of the advantages and disadvantages to each, consent, and where the general law of negligence is able to protect the plaintiff and the defendant. However, in the case of accountants acting as intermediaries in structuring, their role appears more interventionist than in other contexts in that they are given responsibility for converting the plaintiff's expressed future needs into a financial package. An intermediary instructed in this manner has little incentive to deal with life offices which pay no commission or to encourage competition because any commission must then be shared.

3.50 Intermediaries who are empowered to act in a situation of potential conflict will, as fiduciaries, nevertheless owe duties of good faith and must not perform their duties so as to prejudice beneficiaries.[58] The law of negligence imposes a duty of care on the professional which differs from individual to individual according to professional expertise and the circumstances of the case. In general, there is no negligence where reasonable practice which a body of professional opinion would have

---

[57] Interview with Ivor Levy, Frenkel Topping Structured Settlements, 9 December 1991.

[58] See generally P. D. Finn, *Fiduciary Obligations* (1977). See also *Movitex* v. *Bulfield* [1988] B.C.L.C. 104, 120-121.

supported has been followed.[59] In accountancy, the standards laid down by the Institute of Chartered Accountants in England and Wales are regarded by the courts as acceptable as evidence of reasonable practice.

3.51   *Caparo Industries plc* v. *Dickman*[60] affirmed that liability for economic loss due to negligent mis-statement is confined to cases where the statement or advice has been given to a known recipient for a specific purpose of which the maker was aware and upon which the recipient has relied and acted to her or his detriment. Thus, in the context of structured settlements, it may not matter who instructs the intermediary. The *Caparo* conditions appear to be met where an accountant purporting to act for one or both parties gives negligent advice, which the plaintiff clearly relies on by accepting the structure.

3.52   In the light of this, we ask consultees whether they consider that the position of the intermediary in structuring raises special issues falling outside the law of fiduciary duty and of professional negligence and which should accordingly be dealt with in the context of a reform of structured settlements.

3.53   As regards the parties' legal advisers and the extent of the professional duty involved, one solution would appear to be for any such adviser in doubt to instruct other independent financial advisers to double-check a structure proposal. This, of course, may lead to a proliferation of experts and increased costs. The Law Society has drafted a guide for practitioners on structuring,[61] which is general in its terms and is aimed at those unfamiliar with the concept. Obviously, as practitioners become more experienced and confident in dealing with structures, they will be able to judge more readily whether further independent advice is required, and how this affects the professional duty to advise their client in the circumstances of each case. We do not think the matter lends itself easily to rigid rules. Again, we express no view, but ask whether structuring is seen to create special concerns about the role of legal advisers which are not adequately dealt with by the existing law governing their duties to their clients.

---

[59]   *Lloyd Cheyham & Co. Ltd*. v. *Littlejohn & Co.* [1987] B.C.L.C. 303, 313. See also Fiduciary Duties and Regulatory Rules, Law Com. No.124,p. 213, para. 5.4.27, footnote 212 at p. 213 (1992) (hereafter Law Com. No. 124). But see also *Edward Wong Finance Co. Ltd*. v. *Johnson Stokes & Master* [1984] A.C. 296. Our enquiries of the Institute of Chartered Accountants have revealed that there are no special rules dealing with the role of the accountant in structuring, nor is any work currently being carried out in this area.

[60]   [1990] 2 A.C. 605.

[61]   Issued in October 1992.

3.54   The matter of the cost of the service is also complicated and is connected with the question of the independence of the intermediary. At present, some accountants are paid by way of commission on the annuity purchase price,[62] and others by way of time-recorded charging. Payment by commission might encourage an intermediary to recommend an annuity which is not, in fact, in the best interests of the plaintiff or which is not the best the intermediary could find. Any such tendency could be alleviated by a practice of disclosing the amount and source of the commission although this may not solve all of the problems.[63] Further, it may be extremely difficult to check an annuity offer brought back by a broker from life markets about which many practitioners have limited knowledge and which are acknowledged to be highly volatile. Offers remain valid for a very short time. There appears to be strong feeling within the legal profession against intermediaries charging by way of commission.[64] The fear has also been expressed that the possibility of charging by commission will encourage charlatans and incompetents to enter the market.

3.55   It is, however, standard practice for financial advisers to charge commission for their services, particularly where they are asked to broker life insurance. Some of the motivation behind legal practitioners' objections to accountants being able to charge in this way appears to stem from dissatisfaction with the unequal position of solicitors who are obliged to disclose commission to clients in similar circumstances and can only retain such monies if the client consents. However, there is no doubt that the market from which annuities are sought by intermediaries remunerated by commission is clearly restricted by that very fact. It is argued by brokers that there is nothing wrong in payment by commission, or any payment arrangement, provided it is acceptable to the parties involved and, where appropriate, the court. In the present context the concerns about possible lack of independence we have noted may be countered to a degree by increased vigilance from solicitors as the latter gain experience in structuring settlements. Those supporting the practice of payment by commission might say that, provided the plaintiff receives full advice about how the proposed intermediary charges and the alternatives, and all fiduciary duties are met, an informed decision can be made. However, against these arguments, we note that in *Beck v. Plasticisers Ltd*

---

[62]   Frenkel Topping charge 3% in all cases in which a structured settlement is created. There is no fee if no structure results.

[63]   The question of disclosure of commission, which has been the subject of much debate, is discussed in Law Com. No. 124, para. 3.4.19.

[64]   Expressed, for example, at AVMA Lawyers Support Group Meeting, 3 December 1991, London.

(Readicut International plc)[65] accountants instructed jointly to advise both parties on a structured settlement charged fees only and not commission, which they felt would be too high. We are also aware that some larger firms of solicitors are following a policy of not using intermediaries who charge by commission, and rely on their own acquired expertise to a much greater extent.[66]

3.56   Again, we ask whether the practice of charging commission gives rise to particular concern in this context, which should be dealt with in any reform of structured settlements, or whether it is simply an aspect of a wider issue which it would be inappropriate to deal with save in the context of a wider examination of the position of intermediaries and professional advisers. We invite comment on the position of the intermediaries and their remuneration, and the specific questions we have here outlined.

(ii) Disclosure of the annuity purchase price

3.57   The question has arisen as to whether defendants should always disclose to the plaintiff the proposed annuity purchase price. Again, this is related to the extent of the duty owed by the plaintiff's solicitor to the client. It is suggested that disclosure is required to enable the plaintiff to assess whether what is proposed in terms of the annual income will meet her or his needs, and whether it is fair and reasonable compared with what could be achieved using the conventional lump sum method. There is a further more basic objection to non-disclosure, which is simply that the defendant should not be allowed 'to get away on the cheap'.[67] It is argued that if people are to be fully compensated any benefits flowing from a structure should be shared. The response to such arguments is that disclosure should make no difference provided all of the plaintiff's needs are met. These opposing views illustrate clearly the current uncertainty about the nature of structured settlements. If it is accepted that the starting point for negotiating a structured settlement should always be the conventionally estimated lump sum (in other words, if structured settlements are seen merely as a variation of the lump sum), it would follow that legal advisers have a professional duty to establish whether the proposed structure is better than the invested conventional sum. However, if it is accepted that structures alter the focus from entitlement determined in the traditional way to need, it is possible that the ascertainment of the conventional figure should feature to a lesser degree in the solicitor's professional duty. The need to know the proposed annuity purchase price

---

[65]   (1992) 8(6) P. &. M.I.L.L. 41.

[66]   James Hunt Q.C. and Stephen Waine, "The Process of Structuring - Proceedings with Caution",(1992) 136(16) S.J. 386, at p. 387.

[67]   See Fiona Bawdon, "A System Where Both Sides Win?",(1992) 6(6) The Lawyer, 5.

would on this view be a matter for determination in each case rather than an absolute requirement. We welcome consultees' views on these rival views.

3.58 Our provisional view is that it is not essential to know the purchase price in every case. The plaintiff's solicitor has a duty to try to achieve restitutio in integrum. If the plaintiff's future needs will be met by the award the plaintiff will be returned to a position as close as possible to that occupied prior to the accident. In any event, the plaintiff's advisors should be able to ascertain how the market price of such an annuity compares with a lump sum ascertained in the conventional way. Not knowing the actual price simply prevents the plaintiff's advisor from discovering the extent of the saving, if any, made by the defendant on the conventional figure. With respect to the argument that the benefit of any saving made by the defendant should be shared, we point out that the possibility of the saving acts as an incentive for the defendant to seek to settle the matter, in which benefit the plaintiff does share. In reaching this provisional conclusion, we acknowledge that structured settlements do take a needs-based approach and that the conventional figure need not be the starting point. Already it features as much or as little as the parties wish.

3.59 Our conclusions are supported by *Braybrooke* v. *Parker*,[68] where Morland J. had to decide whether the defendants should be ordered to disclose to the plaintiff and to the court the annuity purchase cost to the defendants' insurers prior to the joint application by the plaintiff and the defendants for court approval to a structure. Counsel for the plaintiff argued that because a proposed structured settlement is a bargain and one of the parties (the insurer) is in a strong bargaining position, fairness demanded that the annuity price be disclosed. The learned judge noted that it seemed in all reported cases the annuity purchase cost had been disclosed. However, he held that the one question which had to be answered where approval to a structure was sought was: is the proposed settlement - in this particular case, a structured settlement - in the best interests of this particular plaintiff? In his judgment, it was not necessary for the judge to know what the annuity purchase cost was in order to reach that result. The focus of the inquiry was the overall interests of the disabled plaintiff, not any advantages or otherwise to the defendant. He held that the requirements set out in *Kelly* v. *Dawes*[69] as to the information required by the Court when approval of a structured settlement is sought did not support any need for disclosure of the annuity purchase cost. He also noted that in this case there was a substantial issue on quantum - the parties were not agreed on the likely settlement figure - but held that as a matter of principle this did not matter. It would be for

---

[68]   (Unreported), 22 October 1991, H.Ct, No. 90NJ 3965.

[69]   *The Times*, 27 September 1990; *Kemp & Kemp*, vol. 1, 6A-110.

the judge in such a case to take that issue into account when deciding whether it would be to the plaintiff's advantage to accept the offer of the structured settlement proposed. Further, the learned judge thought it was unrealistic to suggest that the plaintiff's accountant advisers would find it difficult to obtain a figure (albeit in general terms) for the cost of the annuity proposed. Finally, Morland J. considered that if insurers were able to obtain annuities to satisfy properly approved structured settlements at an economical rate, this was in the general public interest, because it would presumably keep premiums down.

3.60 Having provisionally concluded, however, that the purchase price of the annuity need not be disclosed, as long as the plaintiff's needs are to be met, we record our belief that voluntary disclosure may in fact be advantageous to the defendant in that settlement may be facilitated where the plaintiff does not want to enter into negotiations unless she or he is advised that the defendant is acting reasonably. We invite comment on the provisional conclusions outlined above.

(iii) Security

3.61 Some concern has been expressed about the security of structured settlements. Problems have been reported in North America where the life policy and insurance industries have been affected by business failures. In this country we have seen that for the payments received by the plaintiff not to be subject to tax there must be no linkage between the agreement between the plaintiff and the defendant's insurer, and the agreement to purchase the annuity between the defendant's insurer and the life office. The plaintiff must therefore be concerned with the long term position of both these insurance companies.

3.62 The possible collapse of the life company may not give rise to difficulties since, under the Policyholders Protection Act 1975, the general insurer will receive 90% of the policy's worth[70] and will thus have the means to meet most of its obligation to the plaintiff. If, however, the general insurer goes into liquidation, the Policyholders Protection Act 1975 has no application since the plaintiff is not a policyholder of that company and it seems must simply join the list of creditors.[71] It could be said that while

---

[70] Section 10(2). The 1975 Act protects policy holders from the consequences of authorised insurance companies failing to meet their liabilities and finances that protection by levies on the insurance industry. See generally *Colinvaux's Law of Insurance* (6th ed., 1990), ed. Merkin, ch. 22.

[71] The other creditors would accordingly take a share of the proceeds of the policy. Although the contract between the general insurer and the life company is in one sense a contract for the benefit of a third party, the plaintiff, none of the statutory exceptions to the doctrine of privity of contract applies so as to enable direct suit by the plaintiff. The Third Parties (Rights against Insurers) Act 1930, for instance, only applies to liability insurance. We understand, however, that the Policyholders Protection Board has recently advised Frenkel Topping Structured

48

the Motor Insurers Bureau ensures there is some protection for plaintiffs who are victims of road accidents where the defendant proves to be impecunious,[72] there is no similar provision for plaintiffs injured in other sorts of accidents, such as those where an employer is liable, or medical negligence cases.

3.63 The question of whether security is a real problem raises issues that are not confined to structured settlements and which it is not appropriate to explore in the present context. Ultimately the answer depends on the strength of the insurance industry and of the regulatory scheme imposed by the Insurance Companies Act 1982 which provides for margins of solvency and for intervention by the Secretary of State where desirable to protect policy holders.[73] Although it appears that the types of insurers who are entering into agreements at the moment are the major insurers with whom the plaintiff can feel secure over a long period of time, recent heavy losses and the collapse of a large company, London United Investments plc, which is likely to lead to a pay-out by the Policyholders Protection Board of at least £100 million, have led to some concern. However, there is no suggestion at present that the funds of last resort will be unable to meet claims.

3.64 We do not think a law reform issue arises here. It is not possible to insure so as to avoid absolutely any possibility that business failure will destroy the benefits of a particular policy. That would require a line of reinsurance stretching to infinity. The analogy of the Motor Insurers Bureau is inappropriate. The Bureau provides backstop protection where the plaintiff would initially be unable to recover against an uninsured or untraced driver, not where the defendant's insurers become insolvent many years later. We are therefore inclined to the view that the desirability of contingency insurance should be a matter of judgment for the plaintiff and her or his advisers in each individual case, together also with the question of who should bear the costs of such insurance. This would also apply to the individual negotiation of special clauses in the annuity policy

---

Settlements that sums owed by an insurer to a third party pursuant to s. 151 of the Road Traffic Act 1988 and a structured settlement agreement reached by consent and approved by the court would probably qualify for protection under the 1975 Act provided that all applicable eligibility criteria contained in the latter Act are met.

[72] By virtue of its agreement with the Secretary of State for the Environment, already referred to at note 115. The Bureau is a unique piece of extra-statutory machinery incorporated at the instance of insurers transacting compulsory motor insurance business in the United Kingdom. The first agreement it entered into with the Minister of Transport to make provision for cases of injury or death caused by motor cars, where the motorist responsible was uninsured and impecunious, was in 1946. As to the circumstances in which the Bureau now makes payments and its general administration, see *Halsbury's Laws of England* (vol. 25, 4th ed.), paras. 784-790, and E.R. Hardy Ivamy, *Fire and Motor Insurance* (4th ed., 1984), pp. 347-365.

[73] Insurance Companies Act 1982, ss. 32-48, 83-86.

protecting the plaintiff in the event of the liquidation of the defendant's insurer. Further, we think that granting special insolvency status to structured settlement creditors is not justified on current evidence as to general security of insurance contracts. We invite comment on whether the problem of security of structured settlements is seen as a real one and if so, whether any and if so, which, of the solutions proposed are viable.

(iv) Health Authorities

3.65 A number of medical negligence cases have been structured. Until August 1992, all of them were annuity-backed. An 'Options Appraisal' report is prepared for and examined by the Treasury. If an annuity is to be purchased by the Department concerned, the Treasury must approve it as 'unusual expenditure'. The discount to the Health Authority, and the fact that the plaintiff is less likely to run out of funds and to have to revert to relying on NHS care, are weighed against the loss of tax which would have accrued to the state from the tax on the income of a conventional award. Annuity backing was preferred because plaintiffs' advisers had reservations about entering into a long term financial commitment with a Health Authority. But Crown agencies usually self-insure, and in 1992, discussions involving both the Department of Health and the Treasury to facilitate Health Authorities simply making periodic payments as and when they are due, meeting the claim from their own resources, were entered into. The self-funding of structures is seen as financially attractive: there should be cash-flow savings to the Authority and Health Authorities could become like 'miniature life offices', with plaintiffs who die prematurely offsetting those who live into old age.

3.66 On 21 August 1992, a case involving 10 year old Sian Boyd O'Toole became the first medical accident case to be settled by means of a self-funded structured settlement.[74] May J. approved a settlement whereby just over £225,000 was paid to the family and into the Court of Protection as a contingency sum. Merseyside Regional Health Authority are to pay regular sums starting at £20,000 per annum together with lump sums every 5 years based on an initial figure of £5,000, and all payments are guaranteed to be index-linked, paid for as long as Sian is alive, and free from all forms of tax. However, the negotiation of structured settlements on this basis is not straightforward. When faced with the possibility of the Department of Health self-funding structured settlements, some plaintiffs' solicitors have indicated they prefer annuities, but will accept self-funding if the settlement is guaranteed in some way by the government. These difficulties were eliminated in the O'Toole case, but may still create problems in other cases. We understand that the Department of Health is, as a result of this, looking into the possibility of the Secretary of State for Health guaranteeing self-funded structured settlement payments by

---

[74] (1992) 136 S.J. 880.

Health Authorities, which would meet plaintiffs' concerns. We believe that such a development should be encouraged and indeed that consideration should be given to extending it to other Government departments which may be subject to personal injury suits. Government departments should at least be in the position of being able to offer a structured settlement where they have admitted liability in a personal injuries action. This is particularly so in the case of the Department of Health, which has indicated its support for structuring in the past, by offering settlements which were annuity based. Otherwise the plaintiff is disadvantaged in the same manner as outlined in paragraph 3.36 above, through having the misfortune to suffer injury at the hands of a particular type of defendant, and for no other reason. We invite comment on this proposition.

(d) Administration and management

(i) Approval requirements

3.67   Some dissatisfaction has been expressed to us about the current administrative procedures involved in structuring an award. A case may involve obtaining approval of the structure from the Revenue, the Treasury, the judge and the Court of Protection. Where either of the latter two are involved, advance approval from the Revenue is mandatory.[75]   A High Court Practice Note aimed at expediting court approval of structured settlements in personal injury cases has been issued.[76]   It has been suggested that if the requirements specified by the court are met, the court should be empowered to give a general approval which would bind the other bodies involved. We do not believe the approval of the court should bind the other bodies. The process is likely to become less cumbersome now that the Practice Note has been issued, and as parties become more experienced in setting up structures. Further, a number of the requirements set out by each body duplicate those of other bodies and preparation for identical requirements will only have to be carried out once. Finally, we regard it as highly desirable that each body effectively preserves its unique jurisdiction in relation to each case. The approach of each body involved will vary, if only subtly in some instances, because the particular interests being protected simply may not overlap. In this context, adherence to a strict form, determined as adequate by one body, is an inappropriate test of general approval. Potter J. in *Kelly* v. *Dawes*[77] observed that even where the standard

---

[75]   See the procedure laid down by Potter J. in *Kelly* v. *Dawes*, *The Times*, 27 September 1990; *Kemp & Kemp*, vol. 1, 6A - 110, and by the Master of the Court of Protection in (1991) 88(33) Law Soc. Gaz. 15, at 16.

[76]   See [1992] 1 W.L.R. 328.

[77]   *The Times* 27 September 1990; *Kemp & Kemp* vol. 1, 6A-110, at p. 6349.

requirements he had previously set out were met, it would be a matter for individual consideration in every case whether the settlement may be approved as being in the overall interests of the disabled plaintiff, and it may well be that other concerns and queries of the court will need to be satisfied before approval is given. We believe other bodies should not be prevented from bringing their own perspective to what those 'overall interests' might be. We invite comment on this provisional viewpoint.

(ii) Court of Protection fees

3.68 Although it is no part of this exercise to examine the general principles upon which the Court of Protection charges fees, there has been some concern about how to treat payments under structured settlements when calculating fees. The Court of Protection supervises certain structured settlements pursuant to its special jurisdiction.[78] In some respects regular payments under such settlements have the characteristics of income, and as such, fees would be levied under the Court of Protection Rules.[79] Nevertheless, there appeared to be some inconsistency, since the Revenue treats the periodic payments made pursuant to structures as capital. However, if the latter view applied for fee purposes the Court could charge nothing at all in relation to the payments. But the Court and the Public Trust Office would still have carried out work in approving the settlement and supervising the use of the payments. Moreover, this would create an anomaly compared to conventional lump sum awards where regular interest received on the lump sum would be liable to a fee. The Court of Protection was concerned to receive a fair fee to cover the costs of administration in these cases. The result of consultation carried out by the Public Trust Office in 1991 was that most respondents favoured setting the percentage of the annual payments made under structured settlements or similar specified financial arrangements to be taken into account for fee purposes at 50%. At current fee levels, this means about two and a half percent of a payment would be paid as a Court fee if the Court was involved. The Rules have accordingly been changed.[80] We consider that the rule change resolves the uncertainty and recognises the special nature of payments under structured settlements. Although the work of the Court and the Public Trust Office is likely to be at a lower level where a settlement is structured, there is some work or administration involved.

---

[78] The Court of Protection administers settlements as part of the legal framework set out for it in the Mental Health Act 1983 (as amended by the Public Trustee and Administration of Funds Act 1986) and the Court of Protection Rules 1984, S.I. 1984, No. 2035. The Court of Protection and the Public Trust Office manage and administer the property and affairs of patients, people who are incapable, by reason of mental disorder, of doing so themselves.

[79] S.I. 1984, No. 2035.

[80] Court of Protection (Amendment) Rules, S.I. 1992, No. 1899.

(e) Actuarial evidence revisited

3.69 The relationship between the multiplicand, the multiplier and the power of the resulting lump sum to buy a bundle of annuities capable of replacing the lost income stream is central to the development of structured settlements. The question arises as to what happens if the judge computes a multiplier in the usual way assuming a real interest rate of 4.5% and the plaintiff then finds the resulting sum is too small to enable the purchase of an annuity capable of replacing the income stream she or he thought the court had agreed had been lost. This was not a problem in the early part of 1992 because with interest rates around 10% and inflation at around 4.4% per annum the plaintiff appeared to be fairly well protected. But if interest rates were to fall relative to the rate of inflation the cost of the same annuities would rise sharply because the relevant government securities would rise in price. As discussed, real interest rates can vary substantially and this has a very pronounced effect on the gilts market. To offset such changes the courts would have to raise or lower the multiplier but there are no indications they would in fact do this. The problem would be avoided if the courts either took actuarial evidence into account in determining the discount rate or had regard to market evidence of what would be required to purchase an annuity of a given size at a given point in time. The same point is made, in a slightly different way in the statement:

> "In logic and in economics, a defendant ought to be able, without making any conventional lump sum assessment of the claim, to calculate and put to the plaintiff a package which meets his assessed needs. However, we still live in a 'lump sum culture.' Parties are still calculating the lump sum value of the claim for judicial approval where required and then negotiating the form of structured settlement."[81]

This implies that the lump sum is calculated before the annuities are considered. Conceptually this is back to front: the focus of the inquiry should be the annual loss and the decision as to the lump sum made in the light of the cost of replacing that loss. These arguments support our conclusions about the use of actuarial evidence in paragraphs 2.21-2.28 and our view as to the need for disclosure of the annuity purchase price in paragraphs 3.57-3.60 above.

3.70 Finally, it must be said that the courts are already embracing the use of actuarial evidence to a significant degree in their approval and support of structured settlements. Actuarial advice now plays a greater role in the determination of awards but it is a role which is played out behind the scenes within the life offices and insurance companies when the terms of

---

[81] A. Whitfield Q.C., "The basics and tactics of structured settlements", (1992) 142 N.L.J. 135, at p. 136.

structured settlements are being calculated. The actuarial role has effectively been grafted on after the event. It seems somewhat inconsistent for courts to laud the value of structures which are based on complex actuarial calculations and predictions, while at the same time to deny the value of that sort of evidence when calculating the multiplier to establish the extent of loss.

Proposals for Major Reform : Alteration to Principle

Judicial power to impose a structure

(a) Introduction

3.71   The first question is whether the voluntary nature of structured settlements should be supplemented by giving the court either a general power or a specific power, in certain circumstances, to require that an award be made by way of a structure.[82] We preface our remarks by noting that damages are not a discretionary remedy. If the liability of the defendant is established or admitted, the court must award damages as sought.[83] The question of whether or not courts should have the power to impose structured settlements is therefore a question about the method or form of payment. In *Heeley* v. *Britton*[84] Rougier J. had no hesitation in not only approving, but also giving a structured settlement his positive blessing. He added:

>   "The sooner it is possible to award damages on this infinitely less
>   hit and miss basis the better."

3.72   The question of imposition is a fundamental one. We shall consider later (in paragraph 3.75) whether , if the court is to have power to impose a structured settlement that power should be exercisable on the application of one or both of the parties or by the court of its own motion. But it has been argued that if the court were able to impose a structured settlement, against the wishes of the plaintiff, this would breach the established principle that plaintiffs should be able to spend their damages awards as they wish. The corollary of this liberal principle is that plaintiffs should be able to insist on receiving their award in the form of an immediate lump sum payment. Imposition of a different form of award has been

---

[82]   In fact, structures have already received indirect legislative recognition in the Social Security Administration Act 1992, s. 88 (the recoupment provisions referred to below - see para. 4.5.)

[83]   See *McGregor on Damages*, (15th ed., 1988), para. 1. "Damages are the pecuniary compensation, obtainable by success in an action, for a wrong which is either a tort or breach of contract....".

[84]   (Unreported), 19 December 1990 (H.Ct.), referred to in *Kemp & Kemp*, vol. 1, 6A-088.

seen as interference with freedom of contract.[85]   Further, it is argued that it is wrong thereby to introduce paternalism in this area of the civil law when awards of damages in other areas continue to leave plaintiffs in receipt of lump sums which they are free to spend as they wish.   We consider that such arguments are not strong. These arguments assume that the natural process of settlement can only involve lump sums and that this should prima facie not be tampered with. But, as already noted, the lump sum is by no means self-evidently the ideal and only form of damages.[86] The court, in awarding tort damages, has a duty to compensate for the loss suffered. That duty creates a right in the plaintiff to demand that she or he be compensated, but in no sense extends to the creation of a right to demand how the compensation be paid. As to paternalism, it seems inconsistent to reject imposition as paternalistic whilst wishing to enhance structuring in every other way for what are essentially paternalistic reasons. The aim of establishing a life-long, inflation-proof pension for the plaintiff and preventing dissipation is based on a benevolent desire to give security of payment to the plaintiff throughout the anticipated period of the loss. Finally, we share the view of the Pearson Commission that the freedom of choice offered by the lump sum is something which the plaintiff would not have enjoyed if she or he had not been injured and is therefore not an essential part of a system based on restitutio in integrum.[87]

3.73   Further, there are other important reasons, unconnected with paternalism, which may justify giving a court power to impose structures. The court has a duty to award compensation which will put the plaintiff back in the position she or he would have been in had the accident not occurred. It is arguable that the replacement of a lost stream of income by periodic payments and the provision of funds to meet medical and other needs created by the injury as the needs arise does this more effectively than the provision of a lump sum.[88] Moreover, there is an inconsistency in a plaintiff arguing that a particular need exists, such as for an adapted house, and then using the money for something completely different. Even in contract law, where a plaintiff is prima facie entitled to the cost of curing a defect in the defendant's performance, damages will not be assessed on that basis if there is no undertaking or proposal to undertake, or at least circumstances which indicate sufficient firmness of intention, to spend the damages on the cure, and not an extraneous purpose. If the

---

[85]   By the act of interfering with settlements. See *Atiyah's Accidents, Compensation and the Law* (4th ed., 1987), (ed. Cane), p.161.

[86]   Para. 2.1 above.

[87]   The *Pearson Report*, vol. 1, p.123, para. 565.

[88]   See paras. 2.7 - 2.42 above (the disadvantages of the lump sum).

money is not to be spent on the need, then the need cannot be real.[89] The state can also be said to have an additional and valid interest in courts being able to make compensatory awards in a form which may prevent plaintiffs becoming a burden on social security and hence on the taxpayer. The attraction of structures is that they go further than lump sums to facilitate the meeting of specific needs as they arise and, in doing so, replicate, so far as is possible, the compensatory basis on which awards are made.

3.74 We do not go so far as to suggest that plaintiffs should always use their damages precisely as envisaged by the actuarial report upon which the damages claim was made and assessed. That would be impractical and inflexible. It also raises the wider question of whether the state and the court should have more input into how plaintiffs spend damages awards. This question, raising as it does broad issues of principle and more pragmatic considerations concerning the difficulty of enforcing an order that money be applied in a particular way, requires more detailed consideration than can be given in the present context. But we consider that, in the context of structures, in principle it is reasonable to contemplate giving courts power to make orders that would result in compensation being awarded in the form that replicates as far as is possible the basis upon which the award is made. The question is whether allowing the courts to impose structured settlements would in fact successfully do this. Quite apart from concerns of principle, to invest the courts with power to impose structured settlements will have profound effects on both the court system and the process of making out of court settlements. We now turn to consider these important and complex practical questions.

(b)   Effect on bargaining positions

3.75 An assessment of the impact of court imposed structured settlements on the relative bargaining positions of the parties depends on the precise form of the court's power. There are several possibilities.

(i)   Provision that the court only has jurisdiction to order a structure on the application of the defendant. This would mean that a structure could be imposed on a non-consenting plaintiff. The possibility that the defendant could use this power to apply to induce the plaintiff either to take a lesser sum rather than face the possibility that the court will impose an undesired structure, or to settle for an unattractive structure concerns us. We believe there are no compelling reasons to invest only the defendant, who has caused the injury and loss, with the right to apply.

---

[89]   G. H. Treitel, *The Law of Contract*, (8th ed.,1991), p. 838; Megarry V.C. in *Tito* v. *Waddell (No. 2)* [1977] Ch. 106, 332C-D, 333.

However, it might be reasonable to allow the defendant to submit in mitigation that a structure would be in the interests of the parties.

(ii)   Provision that the court only has jurisdiction to order a structure on the application of the plaintiff. Here a structure might be imposed on a non-consenting defendant. The reason for giving plaintiffs the right to apply for a structure is based on the view that it is the plaintiff who has been injured by the defendant, and such a choice returns a form of autonomy to the plaintiff. It might be argued that this would lead to an undesirable alteration in the parties' bargaining position. Plaintiffs would use the threat that they would apply for an undesired court-imposed structure to induce defendants either to offer a larger lump sum than would otherwise be forthcoming or to accept a structured settlement. We feel that so long as the features which are attractive to the defendant, such as the discount, are preserved, the suggested alteration in bargaining positions may not be significant. However, we are hesitant to recommend the creation of any new inequality of bargaining power.

(iii)   Allowing either party to apply for the imposition of a structure would appear to balance the bargaining positions, but might not do so in individual cases. The problems outlined in (i) and (ii) above would still exist.

(iv)   Allowing the court to impose a structure of its own motion in any personal injury case before it would raise a number of serious concerns such as who should pay the costs involved, and how the court would inform itself in order to make choices. Although these problems could no doubt be overcome, we do not believe that such an approach to imposition is either desirable or necessary at this stage.

Our examination of principle and of the effects of imposition on bargaining positions outlined above lends considerable support to the option of granting courts the power to impose structured settlements on the motion of either party to an action for personal damages. We turn now to examine the sorts of questions which would need to be asked to establish the bounds of such a power.

(c) What sort of power to impose?

(i) Form

3.76   The first question relating to a possible power to impose without the consent of one of the parties, is what form it should take. The power could be completely discretionary and capable of being exercised in any personal injury case. Alternatively legislation could impose conditions. A majority of the Pearson Commission recommended that the court should be obliged to award damages for future pecuniary loss caused by death or serious and lasting injury in the form of periodic payments unless it is satisfied, on the application of the plaintiff, that a lump sum award would be more appropriate.[90] In addition to this obligation they recommended that the court should have discretion to make such awards for future pecuniary loss caused by injuries which are not serious and lasting.[91] They believed that the existence of such a discretion would encourage the use of periodic awards in out of court settlements. The Ontario Courts of Justice Act[92] (the Ontario legislation) and the New South Wales Personal Injury Damages Bill 1991,[93] (the New South Wales bill), extracted at Appendix B, provide two further examples of approaches which might be taken. Section 116(1)(b) of the Ontario Act confers jurisdiction on the court to impose a periodic award but no such award can be made if the parties otherwise consent, or if the court considers that, having regard to all the circumstances of the case, the order would not be in the best interests of the plaintiff. The New South Wales Bill gives the court power to impose periodic payments for future economic loss in all awards of damages for death or personal injury not actionable under certain statutes.[94] The court would be authorised but not required to order the purchase of an annuity.

(ii)   Mandatory limits or guidance only?

3.77   It would also be necessary to decide whether mandatory conditions should be imposed on the exercise of any power of imposition. In the Ontario legislation it is mandatory for the court to have regard to certain matters to be taken into consideration when determining the best interests of the plaintiff. They focus on the defendant's means, the plaintiff's plans and

---

[90]   The *Pearson Report*, vol. 1, p. 125, para. 576.

[91]   *Ibid.*, p. 126, para. 580.

[92]   R.S.O. 1990, Chap. C.43.

[93]   Introduced on 1 May 1991. Following an election in the same month, the Bill has not been re-introduced into Parliament.

[94]   Namely: Motor Accidents Act 1988 No. 102 (NSW); Workers Compensation Act 1987 No. 70 (NSW); Dust Diseases Tribunal Act 1989 No. 63 (NSW).

practicability. However, because these matters must be looked at having regard to all the circumstances of the case, the court in fact has a broad discretion. The New South Wales Bill also contains mandatory conditions which focus on the plaintiff's ability to manage and invest any lump sum, the views of the defendant's insurer and such other matters as the court thinks fit. An alternative approach would be to express the limits merely as guidelines which would therefore be of persuasive effect only in fettering a broad discretion but would serve to make the law reasonably predictable and to promote settlements. We are of the provisional view that if the court is to be given the power of imposition it should have a broad discretion but that some guidelines would be desirable.

(iii) Monetary limits?

3.78   A further matter for consideration is whether empowering legislation should contain a monetary limit on the exercise of the power. £100,000 is often expressed as a suitable cut-off point below which it is maintained that the administrative costs do not justify structuring.[95] However, in North America, structures have been reported for as low as $2,000 and we understand that in the United Kingdom the sum of £53,000 has been structured.[96] It is to be anticipated that, as experience of such settlements grows, transaction costs will be lowered and minimum figures for feasible settlements will continue to fall. It follows that there would be dangers in making the jurisdiction to award structured settlements dependent on any monetary limit.

(iv) Life expectancy or incapacity?

3.79   Other limits or conditions could be only to allow the power to be exercised where plaintiffs have an uncertain life expectancy or are likely to live for a long time, where they are already in the higher tax bracket, or where they are unable or unwilling to manage a lump sum themselves. This last mentioned situation has been advanced as the only acceptable occasion when a structure should be imposed against the plaintiff's will and immediately raises questions as to what degree of disability or unwillingness is sufficient. The simple answer would be to require legal disability - the plaintiff would have to be a minor or incapable by reason of mental disorder of managing and administering her or his property and affairs.[97] The law already recognises that the state should be involved

---

[95]   Section 2. of the United States Uniform Periodic Payment of Judgments Act 1990 contains a limit of US$100,000. See paragraph 3.3 and n. 5 above.

[96]   Richard Lewis, "Compensation For Personal Injuries : Prospects for the Future", 31 March 1992, Manchester conference.

[97]   I.e. The requirement to trigger the jurisdiction of the Court of Protection - s. 94(2) of the Mental Health Act 1983 (as amended by the Public Trustee and Administration of Funds Act 1986).

in overseeing asset management in such cases. An additional question which would arise in this context is whether in such cases the power of imposition should be exercised in the face of opposition from the plaintiff's next friend. This solution to the question of what degree of disability justifies a power of imposition against the plaintiff's wishes does not take account of the fact that uncertainty and the threat of dissipation is said to exist in every case, not just those where the plaintiff is legally disabled.

3.80   The various conditions suggested can serve as guidelines to a court making a decision as to whether to exercise its discretion to impose a structure rather than to make a lump sum award. Given the comparative novelty of structuring in the United Kingdom, we find it difficult to select appropriate criteria. We therefore express no view on this matter but invite comment. In fact, we think there are strong practical reasons which might militate against the successful use of a judicial power of imposition, and we now turn to examine these.

(d) Difficulties

(i) The discount

3.81   The first significant question concerns the effect of a power of imposition on the practice of discounting discussed at paragraphs 3.28-3.30. At present there is no simple way of quantifying what the discount should be.[98] The discount is the price of a good which the plaintiff and the defendant can only bargain for from each other. Insurers use their bargaining power to strike a discount. Strictly speaking, if the court could impose a structure, the defendant would not need to be induced to negotiate by any discount and the question arises as to the rationale for any discount at all. Those who argue that the defendant is already in too strong a position would have no difficulty in accepting this. We invite the views of consultees. Would the possibility of a court-ordered structure induce plaintiffs not to settle out of court at all, a development we would not wish to encourage? The alternative is to let the court get involved in the matter of the discount if the parties are ordered to negotiate a discount and cannot agree. The only way to achieve this effectively would be to give the court complete discretion as to the terms and conditions it could impose on the parties. This would make for very uncertain law, at least until rules and precedents were established over time. Again, uncertain as

---

[98]   See Hugh Gregory,(1992) 153(8) Post Magazine : The Insurance Weekly 19, at p. 20, setting out how the discounts are calculated. In *Kelly* v. *Dawes*,(*The Times*, 27 September 1990; *Kemp & Kemp*, vol. 1, 6A-110), the discount was 5.8% of the amount which was structured. *Everett* v. *Everett and Norfolk County Council*, (Unreported), 4 June 1991, (H.Ct.), had a discount of 13.75% and in the case of *Grimsley* v. *Grimsley and Meade*, (Unreported), 28 January 1991, (H.Ct.), the discount was 33%. The general trend appears to be 10 - 15% but larger discounts may reflect difficulties in the plaintiff's case and the desire to settle.

we are about aspects of structuring, including the nature and usage of the discount, we are not sure that the process currently lends itself to the development of suitable rules and precedents.

(ii) Security

3.82 The security of the structure could also become a problem for the court. We have provisionally concluded in paragraph 3.64 above that the protection of the contract between the plaintiff and the general insurer in the long term is a matter upon which plaintiffs and their advisers must satisfy themselves. Therefore, if the structure is imposed on an unwilling plaintiff by a court, it may be thought proper for this duty to fall on the state. It would be unfair and unacceptable to place the plaintiff in the position of having to rely on some other body for payments to meet future needs, without in some way guaranteeing those payments. In most cases, the effective defendant will be an insurance company, and hence to require contingency insurance in any case where doubts arise as to security does not seem so unreasonable. We therefore pose the question for insurers in particular as to whether such a requirement would be unworkable. The alternative is some form of Crown guarantee, which we doubt would be acceptable to the Crown and would create the anomalous position whereby the state would guarantee court-ordered structures, but not those reached by negotiation.

(iii) The position of the intermediary

3.83 What would be the position of the intermediaries who currently provide expert financial and accounting advice, and who search the life markets for suitable annuities? At present it is said that they facilitate settlements but do not act in an adversarial manner. However, the creation of a power of imposition might change this. We invite the views of consultees as to whether this would be the case.

(iv) Costs

3.84 The defendant currently meets the costs of the intermediary and no doubt calculates the discount sought accordingly. It does not seem abhorrent to impose costs on a defendant opposing a structure sought by a plaintiff. However, this assumes that plaintiffs will never oppose structuring and defendants will not seek it. We simply do not know whether defendants currently seek to structure more often than plaintiffs and given that it is now suggested that plaintiffs' solicitors could face questions of professional negligence if they do not at least consider this form of payment of damages, any such assumption appears questionable. Costs also have a potent effect on whether or not a matter is pursued as far as the court at all. Further, the cost to the state of funding a guarantee of security for structures and of general administration to ensure orders are complied with would mean the cost of imposing a structure could be quite considerable.

(v) Review

3.85　Should court-ordered structures or any aspect of them be reviewable? In the Ontario legislation review is possible, but only by consent of all the affected parties, the limits of review being set on such terms as the court considers just. Under the New South Wales Bill either party could apply for variation or termination of the arrangements, to be granted at the court's discretion as it thinks fit having regard to the spirit of this part of the legislation. If the structure can only be ordered in the best interests of the parties and there are guidelines set out to determine what those best interests are, then the exercise of that discretion should be appealable. However, if the structure is ordered against the wishes of one party, this might lead to many appeals with attendant additional costs. In a sense appeals against structures ordered by a court are a form of review although reviewability does not normally refer to this. A right to ordinary review would be used in the same way, carrying with it concomitant expense and the need for a further court hearing. It could therefore increase the burden on the parties and the court system. It must be said, however, that the likelihood of appeal may not in fact be any greater than in many other contexts where the court has a choice of remedies. Yet the special context of personal injuries must not be overlooked. Where an injured plaintiff has waited two to three years before a structured settlement is ordered, the threat of a review application by the defendant might force acceptance of an otherwise unacceptable offer. We consider reviewability in other contexts at paragraphs 3.39-3.46 above and, 3.90 and 5.21 below.

(vi) The comparative novelty of structuring

3.86　Creating a judicial power to impose might be premature since the process of structuring is comparatively new to the United Kingdom. Should it be given time to stabilise in form and operation? The fact that this paper asks many questions about consultees' experiences of structuring is an indication that there is much to learn. We also wonder if the highly technical nature of structuring would be reflected adequately by a simple power of imposition. Our brief study of the use of legislation in other jurisdictions indicates that the legislative regimes embrace, in the main, schemes of periodic payment, which are not the same.[99] There might in

---

[99]　See for example the U.S. Model Periodic Payment of Judgments Act 1990, described at para 3.3 above, and the Ontario Courts of Justice Act, Appendix B. In a letter to the Commission, dated 3 June 1992, Robert F. McGlynn of McKellar Structured Settlements, Canada, states that he suspects the real impact of s.116 of the Ontario legislation has not been all that significant, and that he is not aware of any case where it has been applied. He believes that the major difficulty with the section is that it grants the courts a discretion to order periodic payments but

any event be advantages in deferring legislation empowering the imposition of structuring so that any inherent bias within the system towards the lump sum award will be tempered by experience of the process of structuring awards. The general aim of promoting structured settlements could be met in the meantime by the proposals to improve the existing voluntary regime we have made above in paragraphs 3.23 - 3.70. We think such improvements would ensure that structured settlements are used when they should be and when they would best serve the interests of the parties. Our proposals as to improvements to methods of calculating loss will also strengthen the system within which structuring is developing.

(vii) Structuring non-personal injury settlements

3.87 Finally, a significant and wider question is whether such discretion or power, if granted, should be confined to personal injury cases. On the face of it, it might be said that a power to impose structures should be available as a general remedy.[100] However, as already noted in paragraph 3.33, preferential treatment for the victims of personal injury is justified to a degree because there is a strong public interest in specific needs that would otherwise necessarily be met by the welfare system or public institutions such as the health service being met out of the award over a long period of time. Victims of defamation, conversion or breach of contract are less likely to become dependent on the state because of the wrong done to them and are less likely to have continuing long term future needs. As the focus of this paper is on structures in the context of personal injury, we make no further comment on this aspect.

(e) Provisional conclusion

3.88 We have not formed any provisional view as to whether or not there should be a judicial power to impose structured settlements, and seek the views of consultees on this question. We have stated at paragraph 3.72 that we do not regard the arguments against the imposition of structuring based on freedom of choice and hostility to paternalism as convincing. However, there is a clear need for non-anecdotal evidence on the general tendency to dissipation of awards of damages in the United Kingdom. It is hoped that our empirical research will shed some light on this. In the

---

(cont'd) then sets out no guidelines as to how to order them. The suspicion is that trial judges are less than eager to exercise their discretion on the design of a settlement which requires a certain amount of expertise many judges may feel they lack. The New South Wales Bill, also at Appendix B, facilitates, rather than imposes, structuring, and has not become law.

[100] See Raymond S. Kagels, "Structured Settlements under Superfund", (1992) 4(3) Environmental Claims Journal 349. Kagels notes that in 1987 the U.S. Environmental Protection Agency conducted a study of various alternative funding mechanisms and determined that structured settlements held significant promise of providing settlement incentives for all parties to litigation arising from the Superfund law (CERCLA), passed in 1980 to address the clean-up of closed and abandoned hazardous waste sites in the United States.

meantime, we invite comment on our analysis in paragraph 3.72 of the arguments against a judicial power to impose a structure.

3.89   We have outlined at paragraph 3.73 non-paternalistic arguments from principle based on the greater effectiveness of such awards at achieving the compensatory aims of damages which support a judicial power to impose structured settlements, and seek comment on these. Further, we seek consultees' views as to what criteria might be used to define a judicial power of imposition. A number of possibilities are discussed at paragraphs 3.76 - 3.80. Finally, we seek responses to the difficulties we foresee outlined in paragraphs 3.81 - 3.87. The most important questions are these. Would providing for the judicial imposition of structured settlements be justified given the effects on bargaining positions, administrative difficulties and expenditure of state funds which might be involved? Do we know enough about the operation of structuring in the United Kingdom to seek to set up a power of judicial imposition? Is it better to wait and improve the voluntary regime in the meantime?

Reviewability revisited

3.90   Should the court be able to impose restructuring on a voluntary structured settlement by allowing one or both of the parties to apply to the court for review? We have asked certain general questions about review at paragraphs 3.39 to 3.46. The questions we pose in those paragraphs are also relevant here. It seems unlikely, given our recommendation that review should not lead to reduction of an award, that a defendant would in fact want to apply to a court for review, although the possibility of a future increase might be used at the initial stage to bargain the plaintiff down. We have asked at paragraph 3.89 above whether there should be a power in the court to impose structures. We do not think it would be consistent to recommend that courts be given power to impose conditions of review on structures which have been reached by consent if the courts have no initial power to impose structured settlements. Do consultees consider that judicial power to review structured settlements reached voluntarily is desirable and if so practicable? Our provisional view is that in only one limited area, which does not really amount to imposition in the strict sense, does imposed reviewability seem desirable and possible. Consistent with our previous recommendations, in principle the plaintiff should be able to apply to the court for review of a structured award based on a deterioration in medical condition which has led to financial loss. However, it becomes apparent that such a power would grant access to something very similar to a provisional damages award. We believe, therefore, that the simple answer would be to allow provisional awards to be structured. We discuss this in detail in paragraph 5.21 below, when we look at provisional damages.

Judicial power to impose periodic payments

3.91   We leave aside the larger question of whether the judiciary should have power to grant awards in the form of periodic payments. This is because the focus of this paper has been to look at the enhancement and effectiveness of existing techniques for awarding damages other than by way of lump sum. It may well be, however, that at some stage in the future, the question will be the subject of a specific review.

Alteration to the tax regime

3.92   We have suggested at paragraph 3.33 above that the tax regime be extended to allow life offices to pay instalments of damages direct to plaintiffs, and that the annuities bought by defendants or defendants' insurers to fund structured settlements in personal injury actions be free of tax at the outset. That solution preserves the tax neutrality of the arrangements so that the separate contracts between the plaintiff and the defendant's insurer, and between the latter and the life office, would be maintained. In this way, the solution outlined would remain within the principle of *Dott* v. *Brown*[101] recognised by the Revenue and no element of concession by the Revenue would be involved.

3.93   In order to address this area in the fullest possible manner, we raise for consideration the next logical step in the process. It would be possible to step outside the *Dott* v. *Brown* principle altogether and legislate to extend the tax advantages to the proceeds of all annuities bought, whether by defendants or plaintiffs, with personal injuries damages.[102] This would require a major change to the tax regime. We can see a number of advantages in such a change. The justification for this would be that which we accepted as grounding the rationalisation of the regime which currently supports structured settlements: the desirability of providing security of payments over the period of the loss for the plaintiff who has suffered personal injury, and the removal of the need for the state, and hence the taxpayer, to act as a backstop. Further, the proposal would remove the current problems relating to the discount, since the plaintiff could go into the market and directly purchase a similar package without foregoing the tax advantages. The administrative costs and difficulties deterring or preventing some insurers or bodies from offering structures, would disappear. The plaintiff would be able to rely on the provisions of the Policyholders Protection Act 1975 if the life office collapsed. Finally, we see the proposal as eliminating the problems we outlined above[103]

---

[101]   [1936] 1 All E.R. 543.

[102]   See para. 3.4 above for the position in the United States.

[103]   Paragraphs 2.37 - 2.41.

which the courts currently face in assessing loss when attempting to take account of the incidence of future taxation.

3.94   As to disadvantages, we can see that such a move could be described as further favouring the small percentage of torts cases which involve future financial loss.[104]   The response usually made is that it is these cases which involve very large sums[105] which should be protected if possible. Secondly, it is questionable whether allowing plaintiffs to purchase annuities to fund their own tax-free periodic payments would make best use of the large funds involved in the way currently achieved by structuring negotiations.   There would be no guarantee that the plaintiff would seek out and receive adequate advice, either on future needs or on the best annuity to meet those needs. In fact, the plaintiff would be in the same precarious position outlined in paragraphs 2.31 to 2.33 with regard to investment of a lump sum. It is apparent that part of the attraction of structuring is the forward planning which goes into determining what sort of annuities might be purchased - the change as outlined might detract from the focus on need which we see as positive.

3.95   Connected to this might be a possible return to negotiation and achievement of a settlement figure in the conventional manner, with a consequential loss of negotiation tools where the parties seem to be very far apart, and a consequential loss of savings in time and expense. Our suggestions at paragraphs 2.21 to 2.28 as to the use of actuarial evidence and evidence from the financial markets in assessing loss would to some extent mitigate this undesirable effect.

3.96   It is unclear what would happen to the process of negotiation generally. Defendants might prolong negotiation by holding out for discounts which would allow them to share in the tax savings. However, they could not legitimately claim some portion in savings to cover non-existent administration and cash-flow costs. It seems unlikely that structuring in its current form would simply co-exist with the new option.

3.97   The new regime would require strict policing by the Revenue to ensure that it was not misused for tax avoidance purposes. Because of the justification which we have outlined in paragraph 3.93 above, it would be desirable that the annuities which would now be tax-free were limited to those which are bought on the plaintiff's life, and further, that they be payable only to the plaintiff, and non-assignable and non-commutable by

---

[104]   Identified as 7.5% of all claims in The *Pearson Report*, vol. 2, p. 14, para. 44.

[105]   See Richard Lewis, "Pensions Replace Lump Sum Damages", (1988) 15 J. Law. Soc. 392, at 393.

the plaintiff.[106] While careful drafting of key definitions such as 'personal injury', and development of appropriate forms would certainly be possible, the attendant costs might be too high to justify the benefits sought. We seek consultees' views and comments on the desirability of this proposal.

---

[106] As required in Canada. See Revenue Canada Interpretation Bulletin No. IT-365R2, 8 May 1987, part 5, 24, and Robert G. Watkin, "The New Method of Structuring Settlement Agreements", (1992) 71 Can. B.R. 27. However, assignability from the insurer to a suitable body, in the event of insolvency, would appear to be desirable.

PART IV

INTERIM DAMAGES

Introduction

4.1   In 1968 the Winn Committee recommended the introduction of interim payments out of moneys deposited in court by defendants.[1]   The Committee's reasons for recommending that the court have powers to order such payments were: to accelerate settlements and trials, to provide a model by which negotiations between parties could be conducted in the future, to strengthen the bargaining position of the plaintiff and to relieve hardship.[2]   It would be fair to say the latter reason was accorded some special consideration.[3]   Interim payments in respect of damages are now provided for[4] in Part II of Order 29, rule 11 of the Rules of the Supreme Court, which is set out in Appendix C.   There has been some concern that interim damages are not sought in cases where they might be.   We examine these concerns below.

Proposals for Major Reform: Alteration to Principle

Need

4.2   A major explanation for the under-utilisation of the interim damages procedure is that although the Rules themselves do not require that the plaintiff show a need for the interim payment, it has become customary in personal injury actions for such payments to be limited to sums for which need is shown.[5] Further, the quantum of an interim payment is assessed against the plaintiff's pecuniary losses such as earnings or the cost of special treatment rather than on account of general damages.   These

---

[1]   *Report of the Committee on Personal Injuries Litigation*, (1968) Cmnd. 3691, at p. 38 (hereafter referred to as the *Winn Committee Report*).

[2]   *Ibid.*, at p. 32.

[3]   *Ibid.*, at pp. 29-30.

[4]   Richard Lewis, "Pensions Replace Lump Sum Damages" (1988) 15 J. Law. Soc. 382 at p. 404, also notes the amendment following the Winn Committee recommendations of the Rules of the Supreme Court, to provide for split trials.   By O. 33, r. 4(2A) for the High Court, and by C.C.R., O. 13, r.2(2)(c) for the County Court, the issue of liability can be tried separately from that involving the amount of damages.   This is intended to alleviate some stress for the plaintiff where the medical prognosis remains uncertain.

[5]   *Schott Kem Ltd.*v. *Bentley* [1991] 1 Q.B. 61 (C.A).

requirements have no application to interim payments in other classes of litigation.[6]

4.3 While criticism on the grounds of inconsistency is valid as far as it goes, the reasons for the different requirements seem compelling. One reason for the apparent anomaly is historical, in that the power to make rules of court enabling interim damages to be awarded was first exercised in 1970 in relation to actions for damages for death or for personal injury only. Hence, the scheme was originally operated with this limited subject matter in mind. In 1977 the scheme was extended to provide for such payments in actions for possession of land, and in 1980 the existing much wider power was conferred. The notion of interim payments being to meet a demonstrated need in personal injury cases is in keeping with the original recommendations of the Winn Committee. In *Schott Kem Ltd.* v. *Bentley and Others*[7] Neill L.J. regarded the practice of requiring need to be shown in personal injury cases as sensible, because large interim payments in such cases might lead to difficulties if an order for repayment (necessary where, by mischance, the final damages are less than the interim award) was subsequently made under Order 29, rule 17. The learned judge was clearly recognising the special position of the plaintiff in personal injury cases, where the injury may have caused disability such that a plaintiff who has lost her or his earning capacity and has spent the interim award would find it impossible to make repayment. At the very least, the plaintiff might be disappointed by the final award, particularly if the interim award has already been spent. Further, O. 29, rule 11(1) requires the Court not to risk over-paying the plaintiff, necessitating caution, particularly if there is uncertainty over quantum.[8] It is a relatively simple matter for the Court to exercise the requisite caution by ordering payment of sufficient amounts to compensate the plaintiff for lost wages or other financial hardship up to the anticipated date of trial, and sums needed for special treatment or equipment.

4.4 The *Schott Kem case*[9] was not a personal injury case, and involved the defendant's counsel arguing that the practice of showing need extended beyond such cases. This was rejected by Neill L.J., who noted that the Rules do not in fact prevent an interim payment order being made in the absence of need or prejudice[10]. This could be so in any type of case.

---

[6] R.S.C., O. 29 contains no restriction express or implied to the effect that an interim payment depends on need. See *Kemp & Kemp*, vol. 1, 14-059.

[7] [1991] 1 Q.B. 61, 74B.

[8] *The Supreme Court Practice*, (1991), vol. 1, Part 1, p. 527.

[9] *Schott Kem Ltd.* v. *Bentley* [1991] 1 Q.B. 61 (C.A.).

[10] *Ibid.*, 74C-D.

A discretion has been conferred on the court whether to order an interim payment at all. We think it would be unwise to replace this flexibility with a hard and fast rule unless it is generally felt the discretion is exercised ungenerously. In the light of these considerations, it is our provisional view that the present position should not be disturbed, but we seek comment on whether the discretion conferred on the court to order an interim payment is being exercised ungenerously.

Effect of recoupment of DSS benefits

4.5   There is a complex statutory regime for the recoupment of DSS benefits from tortfeasors which has recently been altered.[11] It has been pointed out to us that the operation of the new provisions can swallow up interim payments, particularly where the latter are small. The result could be that particular interim needs may not be met, thereby defeating the purpose of the exercise to a large degree. One solution could be to give the courts power to order the exclusion of the operation of the new regime in cases where an interim award has been granted for a specific capital expense, for example, the purchase of a specially designed and adapted car, or disability aids. An alternative and more far-reaching solution could be to exclude recoupment in all cases of interim awards. The principle of recoupment would not be subverted in either case since once a final award has been determined, recoupment would apply to the totality, although the time at which repayment is made to the DSS would obviously be deferred. This may also have advantages in terms of simplifying the administrative procedure. A further solution could be to require the defendant's insurer to repay, as part of any interim payment, the benefit paid to date at the time of the interim payment as well as the sum needed for the particular capital item. It might be that such a proposal would be unattractive to defendants, however, reducing the use of the interim regime. We have formed no provisional views on this aspect, and invite responses to the

---

[11]   Section 2 of the Law Reform (Personal Injuries) Act 1948 ("the old regime"), and Part IV, sections 81-104 of the Social Security Administration Act 1992 ("the Compensation Recovery Scheme"), are attempts to deal with the problem of double compensation. They are based on the view that it is not acceptable for a person to receive both state benefits and compensation. The old regime allowed the compensator to deduct from the compensation half of some benefits (for example, Sickness Benefit) which the injured or ill person received, or would have received, for five years after the injury or illness occurred. The amount deducted by the compensator was not paid to the Department of Social Security. The Compensation Recovery Scheme (in force September 1990) means that a defendant paying damages of over £2,500 in respect of an accident that occurred, or a disease that was diagnosed, on or after 1 January 1989, has to pay the amount that the plaintiff has received in "relevant benefits" from the DSS directly to the DSS. The period of deduction runs from the date of claiming benefit to settlement, or five years, whichever comes first. The benefits are deducted in full from the compensation payment and the provisions of the old regime now only apply where the payment is less than £2,500. The Compensation Recovery Scheme applies regardless of whether a claim is settled or litigated and to damages awarded at trial. Periodic payments under a structured settlement are exempt (Social Security Administration Act 1992, s. 88).

question of how often this problem arises in practice, whether it in fact discourages applications for interim awards, and whether, and which of the proposed solutions would be effective.

MIB as defendant

4.6   *Powney* v. *Coxage*[12] established that where the Motor Insurers Bureau is joined as a defendant in a personal injury action, the court has no jurisdiction to order the Bureau to make an interim payment. As already described above[13], where the defendant is an uninsured driver the Bureau has agreed to pay damages due to the plaintiff if judgment is not satisfied in full by the judgment debtor within seven days, subject to certain conditions, one of which is that any such judgment should have been assigned to it. In *Powney* the agreement was judged to give rise only to a potential, not an actual, liability to pay damages. The result in this case was that the plaintiff was unable to obtain an order for an interim payment from either the first defendant or the Bureau. The anomaly, which in this case forced the court to dismiss the appeal with some regret, causes us to invite comment on whether the Rules of Court should be amended specifically to permit orders for interim payment against the Motor Insurers Bureau. Our provisional view is that this should be done.

Proposals for Reform of Existing Regime

Procedural requirements

4.7   The provisions in Part II of Order 29 of the Rules of the Supreme Court are intended to present a means whereby a plaintiff can recover a part of the compensation to which she or he is entitled without having to wait for the trial of the action. However, it is said that whilst the system has become well established, the interim payment is grossly under-used by plaintiffs' solicitors.[14] There are two obvious practical reasons for this. The first reason is that plaintiffs must exhibit the medical evidence in support of the application, thereby placing themselves in a disadvantaged position compared to defendants, who may then strengthen their own reports before disclosing them.[15] The second reason is that the application involves the plaintiff's solicitor swearing what can be a lengthy affidavit and bringing the special damage calculation up to date. This

---

[12]   *The Times*, 8 March 1988,(Q.B.D.); 1988 4(5) P & M.I.L.L. 35.

[13]   Paragraph 3.35.

[14]   John Pritchard *Personal Injury Litigation*,(6th ed., 1989), pp. 67 - 71.

[15]   *Ibid.*, pp. 68 and 71.

extra work may in practice discourage applications for interim payments.[16] However, we believe that it is only fair to defendants that plaintiffs wanting interim damages should by their evidence justify their claim. Do consultees consider matters could be improved by solicitors increasing their efficiency or by simplifying the procedural requirements?

---

[16]   *Ibid.*, at p.71.

PART V

PROVISIONAL DAMAGES

Introduction

5.1   In our 1973 report, we came to the conclusion that we should recommend legislation aimed principally at the sort of case we had called 'chance' cases.[1] It was envisaged that such legislation would provide a procedure to deal with cases in which the plaintiff can prove there is a possibility, but no more than a possibility, that a disease will develop or a deterioration will occur in her or his condition. In such cases the plaintiff can be awarded nothing in respect of the disease or deterioration unless it occurs. Because the Commission was concerned about the uncertainty that would be created as to the defendant's liability by the introduction of provisional awards that permitted a further claim should the disease develop or the deterioration occur, we further recommended that such awards should only be made against certain types of defendants. These were public authorities, defendants insured in respect of the claim, and those not required to have third party vehicle insurance.[2]

5.2   The Pearson Report endorsed these recommendations in general terms[3] and by Section 6 of the Administration of Justice Act 1982, Section 32A was inserted into the Supreme Court Act 1981 establishing a new system of provisional damages.[4] The system came into operation on 1 July 1985, but applies in all cases, including actions commenced prior to that date. The power to award such damages is not confined to the limited class of defendants recommended by the Law Commission. Therefore provisional damages can be awarded against an uninsured person. Only the plaintiff can claim that a provisional damages award be made and an award is final as to immediate damages. The plaintiff can only claim further damages in relation to the occurrence of any 'feared event' specified by the court making the award of provisional damages. Thus, personal injury claims cannot be pursued indefinitely on the basis of unsure prognosis, and

---

[1]   (1973) Law Com. No.56, p.66, para.239. On 'chance' cases, see paras. 2.29 and 2.30 above.

[2]   *Ibid.*, p.66, para. 240.

[3]   The *Pearson Report*, vol. 1, p.127, paras. 584 and 585.

[4]   Set out in Appendix D.

neither can the provisional damages award (immediate damages and interest) be re-opened at a later stage to claim extra damages.[5]

5.3   The courts have thus been given the power to compensate certain categories of plaintiffs whose condition deteriorates. In introducing the reform, Lord Hailsham L.C. did not envisage the procedure being employed very often.[6] The plaintiffs must establish the existence of a "chance" arising at any time in the future that their condition will decline. But the disease developed or deterioration in the plaintiff's physical or mental condition must be "serious". The Practice Direction of 1 July 1985 requires the judge to specify the disease or type of deterioration it has been assumed will not occur for the purposes of the immediate award which will entitle the plaintiff to further damages.[7] Normally, the judge is to also specify the period within which the application for further damages must be made in the judgment.[8] However, R.S.C., O. 37, r. 8(3) allows the plaintiff to apply, within the specified period, for extension of that period. The plaintiff may make more than one such application. Thus, it seems possible that liability could stretch for an indefinite period during the plaintiff's lifetime, a position which defendants do not like.

5.4   The legislation does not define or qualify the words 'chance' and 'serious', though operation of the section appears to turn on how they are interpreted. This, combined with the rare usage referred to by the Lord Chancellor, explains the 1990 dicta of Scott Baker J. in *Willson v. Ministry of Defence*,[9] a case involving deterioration in the plaintiff's physical condition, that "the courts have not yet worked out the precise

---

5   For a general guide to the procedures, see Daniel Brennan Q.C., *Provisional Damages - A Guide to the New Procedures* (1986).

6   *Hansard* (H.L.), 8 March 1982, vol. 428, cols. 28-9. The procedure "will not be invoked unless the plaintiff wants it and the court is satisfied that this procedure will not cause serious prejudice to the defendant".

7   [1985] 1 W.L.R. 961.

8   At the outset, it was thought the courts would generally select a period of five to seven years in the first place. See P.A.Molyneux, "Interviews With Clients By A Worldly Solicitor - Coming Back For More (Provisional Damages)" in (1986) 105 Law Notes 47, at p. 49 and n. 12 therein. In *Mann* v. *Merton & Sutton Health Authority* (Unreported), 15 November 1989, an artificial limit of 30 years was set. The preferred method seems to be not to set a limit at all. See R. Bragg, "Provisional Damages" (1992) 136 S.J. 654 at p. 655.

9   [1991] 1 All E.R. 638, 641d.

circumstances in which awards for provisional damages will be made."[10] The learned judge held that three questions were to be considered:

- whether it is proved there is a chance;
- whether it is proved that there is a chance of some serious deterioration in the plaintiff's physical condition; and
- whether the court should exercise its discretion in favour of the plaintiff in the circumstances of the case.

As to the 'chance' question, the judge held that to qualify as a chance, the possibility must be measurable rather than fanciful. Therefore, a chance may be slim, but still measurable.[11] As to 'serious deterioration', the judge wanted something here beyond ordinary deterioration. Seriousness in any particular case is a question of fact depending on the circumstances of the case. Scott Baker J. held that the section envisaged a clear and severable risk rather than a continuing deterioration. There had to be some clear-cut event, which, if it occurs, triggers entitlement to further compensation.[12] Thus, a threshold test seems to have been created. As to the exercise of the discretion, the judge held that this involved weighing up the possibility of doing justice by a once-and-for-all assessment against the possibility of doing better justice by reserving the plaintiff's right to return. Although there was no discussion of deterioration in mental condition, it is probable that the same approach applies.

5.5   In *Willson v. Ministry of Defence*[13] the plaintiff had injured his ankle at work when he slipped on a polished floor. The injury had left him with continuing disability and pain. Medical reports stated these would be degeneration of the ankle joint, a possibility that the plaintiff would develop arthritis and a susceptibility to further injuries. It was held that the chance element had been satisfied. However, of the three events envisaged, the development of arthritis to the extent of requiring surgery was held not to be serious deterioration, but simply an aspect of a progression of the particular disease. The development of arthritis to the extent of forcing a change in employment was regarded in a similar light. The third event, increased liability to further injury, was held to be entirely speculative as to the nature and gravity of the injury which might be suffered. Serious injury was not to be equated with serious

[10]   [1991] 1 All E.R. 638, 641j-642a.

[11]   *Ibid.*, p.642, a-d.

[12]   *Ibid.*, p.644, e-j.

[13]   [1991] 1 All E.R. 638.

deterioration in physical condition.[14]   Finally, in weighing up what form of assessment would do better justice in the circumstances, Scott Baker J. held that the case fell within the general run of cases where there are uncertainties as to the future. Those uncertainties were of a kind which could properly be taken into account in a once-and-for-all lump sum. He did not therefore exercise his discretion to make a provisional damages order.[15]

Proposals for Major Reform : Alteration to Principle

Gradual deterioration

5.6   The legislation, as interpreted by the case law, has been criticised by the Association of Personal Injuries Lawyers as excluding many cases which involve a gradual deterioration of the plaintiff's condition. It is suggested that provision should be made to permit an award for provisional damages where the trigger mechanism may not involve a specific one-off event, and in cases of natural progression with potentially serious consequences. Our provisional view is that the approach of Scott Baker J. in *Willson* v. *Ministry of Defence*[16] is in keeping with the original recommendations of the Law Commission which were the genesis of the statutory scheme. The Commission referred to the possibility of some event occurring as the distinguishing feature of 'chance' cases.[17] The idea of an 'event' does not stretch easily to include natural progression. On this view, it would require a clear policy reason, such as repeated injustice, to extend the ambit of the section. Accordingly we invite comment on this aspect.

Recovery

5.7   The question has been raised whether the provisional damages regime should be extended to instances where the medical uncertainty concerns the extent to which the plaintiff will **recover** from an already existing

---

[14]   The judge did note, however, that he was satisfied that an injury elsewhere caused (for example, by instability of the ankle leading to the plaintiff falling over and damaging his arm) was at least capable of coming within the section, though this was remote. This had not been shown to be a chance of serious deterioration in the case: *Willson* v. *Ministry of Defence* [1991] 1 All E.R. 638, 643d-f.

[15]   *Ibid.*, p.645a-c.

[16]   [1991] 1 All E.R. 638.

[17]   (1973) Law Com. No. 56, p.66, para.239.

condition.[18] Typical would be psychological or neurological cases and it would be possible to apply the provisional damages regime by assessing the immediate payment by reference to the most favourable medical prognosis, giving the plaintiff the right to seek a further award (perhaps by a certain date) if at the end of the specified period the condition had not improved as predicted by that prognosis. Our provisional view is that, for the reasons given below, this would not be in keeping with the Law Commission's original desire to provide certainty in chance cases.

5.8   It must be acknowledged that although not mentioned in the Law Commission's original recommendations, uncertainty about recovery could in a sense be said to be a 'chance' case. If assessment is made on orthodox lump-sum principles, the chance of recovery from the condition will be taken into account by a suitable percentage reduction in the award. Therefore, if the recovery does not occur or occurs earlier or later, the plaintiff has been under or over-compensated, and cannot make this up in any way by pursuing a further damages award. Applying a type of provisional award regime would correct the difficulty. However, we do not believe such an approach is desirable. The regime currently allows an initial payment based only on the existing situation, which is therefore made as certain as it can be. Uncertainty surrounding deterioration is then ameliorated by being dealt with in the future when that uncertainty is resolved. Turning this process on its head so that the initial payment would be based on the most favourable medical prognosis, with a right to return for more if that prognosis proves to be incorrect, would restore uncertainty to the first award, and possibly encourage malingering to found a further application. It would seem better to base a right to return for more on clear deterioration rather than failed recovery. Aside from the problem of malingering already discussed, we wonder whether the types of cases involved would raise further practical difficulties, which are insurmountable. It might be much more difficult for experts to give dates around which specified periods could be built. Predicting recovery is quite different from predicting deterioration, especially where psychological and neurological conditions are involved. Further, lapses in recovery are common in such instances. Finally, a defendant may feel hard done by when recovery occurs earlier than predicted, and justified in requesting some sort of refund. Yet it would usually be highly undesirable to allow such recovery, as the plaintiff may be in no position to repay. We invite comment on these aspects and on our provisional view that the regime should not be extended.

---

[18]   See Richard James, "The Provisional Damages Rules - Some Criticisms", (1986) 136 N.L.J. 231.

Proposals for Reform of Existing Regime

Introduction

5.9 There are four features of the existing regime which might be considered for possible reform. These concern the time limits for applying for additional damages, the courts' overriding discretion to grant a provisional damages order, the limited entitlement to make one application for further damages in respect of each disease or type of deterioration specified in the provisional damages order, and the effect of the provisional damages regime on actions by dependants under the Fatal Accidents Act 1976 and by the estates of deceased persons under the Law Reform (Miscellaneous Provisions) Act 1934.

Time limits

5.10 The time limits to apply for additional damages could be seen as unnecessary on the basis that it should be anticipated the court will be asked to extend the time limit if the specified period is due to expire and no application has been made. This is based on the view that the court may well grant the request. We do not agree with this argument. As a matter of principle, it could prejudice the defendant in some cases to leave the period indefinite, and this reasoning was considered very important by the Law Commission in making our original recommendations. In addition, there are many practical reasons why a specified period is preferable, and may in fact be advantageous to both parties. There will be very few cases where the medical experts will not be prepared to name a date by which the event leading to deterioration will occur. If that date passes without deterioration, it is likely the risk of occurrence will have diminished, and new medical reports will be able to establish a new period with reasonable clarity. The risk may even have fallen so much that it will be appropriate for the court to exercise its discretion **not** to grant an extension of the original period. It therefore cannot be assumed either that the plaintiff will automatically seek an extension, or that the court will grant it as a matter of course. If the extension is granted, and the risk reduced, the defendant will be able to re-assess the extent of insurance cover which needs to be renewed. Further, both parties, though the plaintiff in particular, and the plaintiff's solicitor, have a particular date to work to for monitoring of the medical condition, and for keeping of records. The court, which has a pure record-keeping duty, is also liable to maintain a file which is reasonably up-to-date. It is simply less likely that the claim will be forgotten, and this is especially important where the 'chance' event takes years to happen. Finally, R.S.C., O.37, r. 8(2) is a flexible provision in any event, allowing the judge not to specify a time limit where this is seen to be appropriate. The courts are making ample use of this discretion.[19] We see no reason to replace this flexibility with a rigid rule.

The court's overriding discretion

5.11   The second relevant feature of the regime concerns the court's overriding discretion to grant a provisional damages order. Is this power too wide? R.S.C., O.37 r. 8(1) provides that the court "may" make an award of provisional damages, and this is the discretion referred to by Scott Baker J. in the *Willson* case[20] as the third step once the plaintiff has overcome the hurdles of 'chance' and 'serious deterioration'. It might be thought that leaving the discretion with the court simply creates a further uncertainty in an already difficult area of the law. However, on balance, we believe that the discretion ensures flexibility and is therefore the most appropriate machinery for dealing with existing uncertainties. Further, the court should be allowed to take prejudice to the defendant into account.[21]

Only one application

5.12   Under R.S.C., O.37, r. 10(6), a plaintiff is only entitled to make one application for further damages in respect of each disease or type of deterioration specified in the order for the award of provisional damages. It appears that this could create injustice where, for example, two limbs are injured in an accident, leaving a risk that both will develop arthritis at a later stage. Since it is the disease which must be specified, and not the susceptible body parts, if arthritis developed in a leg first but in an arm later, the plaintiff cannot claim further damages for the latter having already claimed for the former. It does not appear to us to be appropriate to deal with such a factual situation by delaying the claim for the first deterioration until the second manifestation arising from the same injury occurs. The plaintiff may need funds when the first manifestation occurs and the second event may never occur. The plaintiff would be placed in a distressingly uncertain position. This possible effect of r.10(6) also seems to go against the general wording of section 32A(1) of the Supreme Court Act 1981.   The logic embodied in r.10(6) of protecting the defendant is apparent. However, in the circumstances outlined it seems unduly harsh. One solution would be to give the court more discretion by empowering it, when approving the original provisional award, to allow for additional applications for further damages, or to regard a second application arising from the same injury, though based on the same

---

[19]   See n. 8 above.

[20]   *Willson* v. *Ministry of Defence* [1991] 1 All E.R. 638.

[21]   As suggested in Daniel Brennan Q.C., *Provisional Damages - A Guide to the New Procedures*,(1986) at p.52.

deterioration, to be seen as part of the same application. Alternatively the court could have power in hearing the further application specifically to permit a further application again based on the same deterioration. It is to be expected that such powers would be exercised very rarely. We are inclined to the view that such a provision would more fully reflect the spirit of the legislation, and invite general comment on it, but in particular, on whether such difficulties have arisen in practice, and to what degree.

Fatal Accidents Act 1976 and the Law Reform (Miscellaneous Provisions) Act 1934

5.13   A significant question has arisen, concerning the effect of the provisional damages regime on actions by dependants under the Fatal Accidents Act 1976 and by the estates of deceased persons under the Law Reform (Miscellaneous Provisions) Act 1934.   Where a living plaintiff in a personal injury action obtains an award of provisional damages and has the right to apply to the court for further damages should she or he develop some specified disease or diseases or deterioration in health, but then dies as a result of such specified disease or deterioration before a claim can be brought for further damages or before it can be pursued to judgment, is a claim by the dependants under the Fatal Accidents Act 1976 precluded by reason of the provisional award, even though no further award has ever been made?   The matter has not been adjudicated by the Court of Appeal or the House of Lords, although it has been the subject of a judgment by the former in *Middleton* v. *Elliott Turbomachinery Ltd.*[22]

5.14   An award to dependants under the Fatal Accidents Act 1976 can include as much of the deceased's potential earnings in the lost years as would have gone to support the dependants. The courts have held that the right to bring a Fatal Accidents Act claim is lost if the deceased made a claim in respect of the same injury during her or his lifetime where the claim has been settled or gone to judgment.[23] We think this conclusion entirely correct.   The problem concerns the meaning of 'settled or gone to

---

[22]   *The Times* 29 October 1990; (1990) 6(8) P. & M.I.L.L. 58-59; (1991) 7(1) P. & M.I.L.L. 4-5.

[23]   *Read* v. *The Great Eastern Railway Co.* (1868) L.R. 3 Q.B. 555.   Section 1(1) of the Fatal Accidents Act 1976 provides:-

'If death is caused by any wrongful act, neglect or default which is such as would (if death had not ensued) have entitled the person injured to maintain an action and recover damages in respect thereof, the person who would have been liable if death had not ensued shall be liable to an action for damages, notwithstanding the death of the person injured.'

Read interpreted the extent of the new action permitted by the equivalent section in the Fatal Accidents Act 1846 (which, for all intents and purposes, contained almost identical wording).

judgment'. If a provisional award (the immediate payment) is seen as a final determination of the rights of one party against the other, it seems possible that a claim for any part of the lost years' earnings could disappear altogether, because it cannot be saved by the Law Reform (Miscellaneous Provisions) Act 1934. The latter was amended by the Administration of Justice Act 1982, s. 4(2)[24] to provide that a surviving cause of action vested in a deceased person's estate now excludes any lost years element. The amendment was motivated by a desire to prevent non-dependant heirs receiving a windfall,[25] but could have the consequences outlined above if the nature of provisional damages awards is not clearly defined. A plaintiff, in deciding whether to seek an award of provisional damages together with the specification of a feared event which might lead to the death of the plaintiff, is faced with the possibility that she or he may later have to make an urgent and distressing application although then in a terminal condition, in order to preserve the claim to compensation for the lost years. In contrast, if the plaintiff does not seek provisional damages, in the award of lump sum damages she or he would be able to receive compensation in some degree for the possibility of the occurrence of the feared event.

5.15 This was exactly the factual situation in *Middleton* v. *Elliott Turbomachinery*[26]. The trial judge made an immediate award, and, under O. 37, r. 10 of the Rules of the Supreme Court, declared that if the plaintiff developed any of the specified conditions he would be entitled to apply for further damages. He also declared that the part of the judgment which gave the plaintiff a conditional right to apply for further damages at a future date was not a judgment or satisfaction as precludes such a claim by his surviving dependants under the Fatal Accidents Act 1976 for

---

[24] The amendment is now s.1(2)(a)(ii) of the Law Reform (Miscellaneous Provisions) Act 1934. Sections 1(1) and 1(2)(a)(ii) provide:-

> (1) Subject to the provisions of this section, on the death of any person after the commencement of this Act all causes of action subsisting against or vested in him shall survive against, or as the case may be, for the benefit of, his estate ...

> (2) Where a cause of action survives as aforesaid for the benefit of the estate of a deceased person, the damages recoverable for the benefit of the estate of that person:-

> (a) shall not include -

> ... (ii) any damages for loss of income in respect of any period after that person's death.

[25] See *Hansard* (H.L.), 8 March 1982, vol. 428, col. 28, speech of Lord Hailsham L.C., introducing what is now the Administration of Justice Act 1982, in the House of Lords.

[26] *The Times*, 29 October 1990.

damages corresponding with such further damages. However, the Court of Appeal did not think such a declaration could be made. Mustill L.J. stated that it was no part of an appellate court's function to act as a purveyor of advice by expressing opinions on events which, if they happened at all, would happen in the future, and were more likely not to happen than to happen. Further, if a claim did arise from the happening of that event, it would be brought by persons not party to the present actions and whose identity could not accurately be predicted now. Therefore there was no ground for the court below to intervene by granting the declaration. It was seen as significant by the Court of Appeal that the plaintiff had had a choice: to an immediate but small award in relation to the risk that serious consequences would ensue, or to an immediate award of provisional damages with a right to return should he become ill. The court declined to express a view on the substantive issue.

5.16   The plaintiff had also sought a further declaration that on his death any right to an award of further damages under the judgment would devolve upon his estate and that the limitation imposed by section 1(2)(a)(ii) of the Law Reform (Miscellaneous Provisions) Act 1934 was not to apply to such an award for further damages. But although that further declaration was not pursued before the judge at first instance, the point which was the subject of that declaration was before the Court of Appeal. The Court of Appeal expressed the tentative view that the position was not different from any other judgment for damages to be assessed and that consequently in assessing those damages the court would be able to take account of any loss of earnings attributable to the shortening of the plaintiff's life due to the occurrence of the 'feared event' referred to in the provisional award. That view was expressed obiter and, as we understand the position, the point had not been argued, so some doubt remains whether it is the law.

5.17   The questions which remain unanswered therefore are:

(a)   Is the award a final determination so that no further claim can be brought by dependants under the Fatal Accidents Acts where otherwise appropriate?

(b)   Is a claim by the estate for earnings in the lost years barred by section 1(2)(a)(ii) of the Law Reform (Miscellaneous Provisions) Act 1934?

5.18   As to (a), we would merely comment that we do not see a provisional damages award as final and conclusive of the parties' rights. The further damages stage is not merely a matter of assessing damages already agreed to be paid at the initial stage. There are strict rules of notice to allow the defendant to meet the claim. This may be done by challenging the plaintiff's contention that the chance condition has occurred and is the result of the defendant's negligence. Effectively the medical condition is still in dispute between the parties. There may also be raised a suggestion of duplication between the provisional damages and the further damages claim, or of disability unrelated to the cause of action. Most importantly, R.S.C., O. 37, r. 8(3) gives an overall discretion to the court to grant extensions of time periods within which applications for further awards must be made. Because prejudice to the defendant will be one of the matters to which the court will attend in the exercise of this discretion, it cannot be said that the immediate award of provisional damages determines once and for all the rights of the parties. Therefore, we are inclined to the view that a provisional damages award does not fall foul of the rule in *Read* v. *Great Eastern Railway Co Ltd.* [27] To view the matter otherwise would be to defeat the purpose of the provisional damages scheme, and create inconsistency. A terminal condition, if it advances quickly enough, could prevent dependants of a deceased person from pursuing compensation which, conversely, a serious deterioration would allow the victim to pursue by completing the claim begun in a provisional damages action. Rights and liabilities should not fall to be determined by capricious acts of fate. However, in the absence of a determination by the courts, uncertainty exists which it was intended the provisional damages regime would remove.

5.19   As to (b), we respectfully agree with the obiter view of the Court of Appeal in the *Middleton* case that section 1(2)(a)(ii) of the Law Reform (Miscellaneous Provisions) Act 1934 does not prevent a claim by the estate for earnings in the lost years. Again, however, particularly since we understand the point was not argued, until this matter is the subject of an actual decision and pronounced on by the court, uncertainty prevails.

5.20   Our provisional view is that this uncertainty is not something which either plaintiffs or defendants should live with until there is a judicial decision in a suitable case. Indeed, it seems distasteful that a plaintiff with a terminal condition may have to pursue a last-minute action to determine the matter. In the meantime, there will be numerous actions involving plaintiffs having to decide whether or not provisional damages are appropriate for them, although the risk of a terminal condition developing may be many years off. In such circumstances, it will be very difficult for legal advisers to give proper advice. The result might be the under-utilisation of the provisional damages action. All of these effects are undesirable. The solution would appear to be to legislate specifically to provide that dependants can pursue further damages actions based on provisional damages awarded to a plaintiff before a reserved terminal condition manifested itself and prevented the plaintiff pursuing the further award because of earlier death. This would remove the provisional damages regime from the ambit of Section 1 of the Fatal Accidents Act

---

[27]   (1868) L.R. 3 Q.B. 555, para. 5.14 above.

1976. We invite comment on this proposition and the reasoning behind it.

Structuring provisional awards

5.21 A final difficulty which arises with the regime as it currently exists is that provisional awards of damages cannot currently be structured, as they result from a court judgment and therefore do not attract the tax concessions. As outlined in paragraph 3.90 above, we think that this form of reviewability is desirable and practicable, such that provisional, and indeed, interim awards, should be able to be structured where both parties consent. Such reform would require the Revenue to recognise court orders facilitating structured interim and provisional awards as a type of 'Model Agreement', and possibly amendment to both the statutory interim and provisional damages regimes. We prefer this approach to allowing some sort of special review for structured settlements because it is desirable to build comprehensively on the existing system, and because there can then be no suggestion that structures are being treated as a special case. The concept of reviewability we favour has already been recognised by the law as desirable for lump sum awards, and it is anomalous that structures should not also be included. The statutory schemes provide reasonable limits to reviewability which protect both plaintiffs and defendants. In the context of this provisional recommendation, upon which we invite comment, the answers to the questions we have posed about interim and provisional awards in Part IV and this Part become very important, as we would wish the regimes to be adopted as often as is appropriate.

PART VI

PROVISIONAL CONCLUSIONS
AND SUMMARY OF CONSULTATION ISSUES

6.1   We have considered:

(i)   the nature of lump sum damages, and whether current methods of assessment can be improved; and

(ii)   the development of structured settlements, specifically:
(a)   proposals to improve the existing regime, covering rationalisation of the tax regime, the need to monitor the negotiation process and administration and management;
(b)   whether courts should have the power to impose a structure against the wishes of both or one party;
(c)   whether courts should have power to review voluntary structured settlements; and
(d)   whether the existing tax regime should be extended; and

(iii)   the operation of the interim damages provisions, in particular :
(a) the requirement to show need, the effect of recoupment of DSS benefits, and the position of the Motor Insurers Bureau as defendant; and
(b) whether the procedural requirements can be simplified; and

(iv)   the operation of the provisional damages provisions, in particular:
(a) whether the regime should be extended to cover gradual deterioration in the plaintiff's condition and cases in which the uncertainty relates to recovery rather than deterioration; and
(b) whether changes should be made to a number of aspects of the existing regime, including the time limits for applications for additional damages, the court's overriding discretion, the plaintiff's entitlement to make only one application in respect of each disease or deterioration, the effect of the provisional damages regime on proceedings under the Fatal Accidents Act 1976 and the Law Reform (Miscellaneous Provisions) Act 1934, and the structuring of provisional awards.

We shall now set out the issues on which we seek the views of consultees and our provisional conclusions.

Lump Sum Damages - Actuarial Evidence

6.2   We provisionally conclude that actuarial evidence should receive greater judicial recognition, and that this should be facilitated by formalisation through appropriate legislation which will remove the need for actuarial tables to be proved in each individual case (paragraph 2.22).

6.3 In conjunction with the conclusion outlined above, we believe that courts should make more use of information from the financial markets in determining the appropriate rate at which to discount multipliers to take account of the fact that a lump sum has buying power today. Accordingly, we seek consultees' views as to whether it is possible to use evidence of the return on Index-Linked Government Securities at the date damages are assessed as a guide to the real return on investment before setting multipliers, and whether such evidence would be less arbitrary than assuming a conventional rate of 4.5%. We also seek consultees' views as to alternative indicators of real rates of interest (paragraphs 2.23 and 2.24) and as to how much weight should be given to such evidence. If it is more reliable than the conventional 4.5%, we favour the legislative instruction being mandatory (paragraph 2.25).

6.4 We outline, in order to stimulate discussion, a proposal to decouple the court's role in identifying loss from its role in commuting the loss into a single lump sum of damages. By this, the court would in effect assess the valuation of loss by the financial markets, and would itself only take the prior step of establishing the annual loss and the number of years over which the loss could be expected to continue. We express no view about this proposal, but seek comments on it (paragraphs 2.26 to 2.28).

6.5 We outline the position with regard to lump sum assessment and taxation. We propose no change to the rule in *British Transport Commission* v. *Gourley*[1] (paragraphs 2.37 to 2.39).

6.6 We examine the approach to future taxation in *Hodgson* v. *Trapp*[2] and suggest that the reasoning may be open to question. We suggest that our proposals outlined at paragraphs 2.21 to 2.28, and 3.92 to 3.98 may provide solutions. We invite comment on our analysis (paragraphs 2.40 and 2.41).

6.7 We note that the general rule is that future inflation is to be ignored in the assessment of lump sum damages for future loss. We conclude that our proposals as to the use of actuarial evidence and evidence from the financial markets will have a positive effect in providing for future inflation to some degree (paragraph 2.42).

---

[1] [1956] A.C. 185.

[2] [1989] A.C. 807.

Structured Settlements

Rationalisation of the existing tax regime

(a) Loss in cash flow to insurer

6.8   We invite comment on whether the fact that the life office has to pay tax on the annuity payments it makes to the general insurer, which must then gross up the payments it makes to the plaintiff, only claiming back those payments after 12 - 18 months, is a significant disincentive to defendants considering whether to offer a structured settlement. We provisionally conclude that the problem may be overstated. However, we pose the question whether, even if there is no disincentive, the defendant or the defendant's insurer should have to bear the loss of cash-flow at all, given that the Revenue has recognised the economic and social advantages of structuring (paragraphs 3.25 and 3.26).

6.9   We suggest that if there is a real disincentive, or if the question we have posed is answered in the negative, the answer may be to enable the life office to make payments direct to the plaintiff without prejudicing the tax position of such payments and requiring the defendant insurer at the same time to guarantee such payments. We invite comment on this proposition (paragraph 3.27).

6.10   We seek comment on the nature of the discount sought by defendants on the annuity purchase price, specifically, whether it is to cover the administrative costs outlined above, or also is to permit the defendant to participate in the tax benefits accruing to the plaintiff. If the latter we ask whether it is legitimate for the defendant so to participate (paragraph 3.30).

(b) Non-trading insurers

6.11   We seek comment as to what extent non-trading insurers are prevented from offering structures because they cannot set-off gross-ups in payments to plaintiffs against corporation tax. We conclude that if the problem is significant, the Revenue could allow tax to be reclaimed in specified instances. However, we favour the solution already outlined, of allowing the life office to pay instalments of damages direct to the plaintiff, thereby removing the need for the general insurer to gross-up payments at all. We conclude that in order for the plaintiff to receive the full amount of the payments, it would be necessary for the Revenue to extend the tax-free status currently given to structured settlements to all annuities purchased by defendants or defendants' insurers in actions for personal injury or under the Fatal Accidents Acts. We do not go further and recommend the extension of the tax reform suggested to annuities purchased with other kinds of damages award (paragraph 3.33).

(c) CICB and MIB

6.12   We provisionally recommend that the uncertainties surrounding the ability
        of the CICB and the MIB to offer structured settlements be removed as
        soon as possible. We believe that provided these bodies are put in the
        position of being able to purchase suitable annuities, the solution outlined
        in paragraph 3.33 should eliminate most difficulties (paragraph 3.36).

(d) Court-ordered structures

6.13   We conclude that at least where the parties consent, the court can
        currently order a structure. However, we note that the favourable tax
        regime only applies where the parties have reached agreement and all legal
        proceedings have been discontinued. Therefore, there is no incentive to
        seek a court-ordered structure. We provisionally recommend that the
        favourable tax regime should extend to structures ordered by a court with
        the consent of both parties (paragraph 3.37).

6.14   We provisionally recommend that the judicial power to award damages
        in the form of a structure where both parties consent, be enshrined in
        legislation, to remove all uncertainty (paragraph 3.38).

(e) Reviewability

6.15   We seek comment on whether the device of the contingency fund is seen
        as adequate to deal with changes in the plaintiff's circumstances that arise
        after the creation of a structured settlement (paragraph 3.39).

6.16   We provisionally conclude that review is desirable in principle, to the
        extent of taking into account any deterioration in the plaintiff's medical
        condition connected with the original injury, provided it has caused further
        financial loss. We do not think improvement in the plaintiff's condition
        should trigger reviewability, nor that structures should reviewable to take
        account of inflation (paragraph 3.42).

6.17   We consider whether reviewability should be provided for in voluntary
        structures, and consider the two forms reviewability could take - the
        provision of new money, or restructuring of the original agreement. We
        note that the provision of new money would not appear to attract the tax
        benefits under the Model Agreements (paragraph 3.44). However, we
        conclude that it seems doubtful defendants would agree to reviewability in
        this form even if tax law was amended. Costs would also seem to be a
        deterrent. Restructuring of the original package without provision of new
        money is currently possible within the existing tax regime, but we
        conclude that this appears to be undesirable both in principle and practice
        (paragraph 3.45). We provisionally conclude that to amend the tax

legislation is not likely to lead to the greater use of voluntary reviewable settlements, but we invite comment on this (paragraph 3.46).

The need to monitor the negotiation process

(a) The position of the intermediary

6.18 We pose questions about the position of intermediaries such as accountants. We ask whether accountants should be able to act for both parties, what the extent of their duties are and whether the fact that the plaintiff has legal advisers who should supervise the settlement is inadequate protection (paragraph 3.48).

6.19 We then ask of consultees in summary whether they consider that the position of intermediaries in structuring raises special issues which fall outside the law of professional negligence, and which require reform (paragraph 3.52).

6.20 We ask whether structuring raises special concerns about the role of the solicitor which are not accounted for within the ordinary law of professional negligence (paragraph 3.53).

6.21 We ask whether the practice of intermediaries charging commission for their services is commensurate with their duties as envisaged and again, whether the ordinary law of professional negligence cannot provide adequate protection for plaintiffs (paragraph 3.56).

(b) Disclosure of the annuity purchase price

6.22 We provisionally conclude that there should be no requirement that the defendant or defendant's insurer disclose the cost of the annuity which forms the basis of a structured settlement, so long as the plaintiff's needs are met. However, we note that it is unlikely the plaintiff will come to the bargaining table and agree to a settlement advantageous to both parties unless the defendant is seen to be acting reasonably by voluntarily making such disclosure (paragraphs 3.57 to 3.60).

(c) Security

6.23 We ask for comment on whether security of structured settlements is regarded as a real problem. We provisionally conclude that it is impossible to insure so as to avoid absolutely the possibility of business failure. We also conclude that contingency insurance, or the inclusion of special protective clauses in the annuity policy, are matters which should be considered by individual plaintiffs and their advisers. We consider that present evidence does not justify alteration to insolvency laws to provide structured settlement creditors with special status. (paragraphs 3.63 and 3.64).

(d) Health Authorities

6.24 We note that the Department of Health has offered structures in the past which have been annuity-backed. We also note that the Department now shows a preference for self-funded structures, and that this has created difficulties relating to security which are currently being negotiated, and which have been overcome in at least one recent case. We welcome the current moves to facilitate Government Departments being able to enter into and guarantee self-funded structured settlements where they are defendants. We see no reason why a plaintiff should be disadvantaged by suffering personal injury at the hands of a particular class of defendant and for no other reason, particularly where that defendant offered structured settlements in the past (paragraphs 3.65 and 3.66).

Administration and management

(a) Approval requirements

6.25 We provisionally conclude that where approval of a structure is required of a number of bodies, such as the Revenue, Treasury, the High Court and the Court of Protection, the court should not be empowered to give a general approval which would bind the other bodies involved (paragraph 3.67).

(b) Court of Protection fees

6.26 We outline the new Court of Protection Rules setting fees in relation to its administration of structured settlements (paragraph 3.68).

Actuarial evidence and structuring

6.27 We examine actuarial evidence again in the light of its use in structuring, and note that courts are accepting the use of actuarial evidence in accepting structures (paragraphs 3.69 and 3.70).

Judicial power to impose

6.28 We examine freedom of contract and anti-paternalism arguments which reject judicial imposition of structuring, and conclude these are not persuasive (paragraph 3.72).

6.29 We advance two further arguments which we conclude justify in principle that courts should have power to have more input into how plaintiffs spend damages awards for future care and loss of earnings. We pose the question whether power to impose structured settlements would in fact achieve this (paragraphs 3.73 and 3.74).

6.30 We examine the effect which a power to impose might have on bargaining positions, and conclude that this suggests considerable support for a judicial power to impose structured settlements on the motion of either party to an action for personal injury (paragraph 3.75).

6.31 We pose a series of questions designed to establish what sort of power to impose structuring would be preferred, if enacted (paragraphs 3.76 to 3.80).

6.32 We then examine what we consider to be strong practical obstacles to a judicial power to impose structuring at this time (paragraphs 3.81 to 3.87).

6.33 We seek comment on the arguments from principle which support a judicial power of imposition. We also seek consultees' views on the criteria which would define such a power. Finally, we seek responses to the practical difficulties which could currently present judicial imposition (paragraph 3.89).

Judicial power to review

6.34 We ask of consultees whether a judicial power to review structured settlements reached voluntarily is desirable and practicable. We provisionally conclude that review is immediately possible in relation to provisional awards in any event (paragraph 3.90).

Judicial power to impose periodic payments

6.35 We leave aside the question of whether there should be a full blown legislative system of periodic payment of damages, on the basis that such consideration would be premature (paragraph 3.91).

Alteration to the tax regime

6.36 We raise for consideration a major change to the tax regime which would involve stepping outside the *Dott* v. *Brown* principle, by allowing all periodic payments made under annuities bought either by plaintiffs or by defendants with personal injury damages to be tax-free. We suggest the annuities only be those bought on the plaintiff's life, and payable to the plaintiff, being non-assignable and non-commutable. We outline the advantages and disadvantages of such a proposal and ask for comment without expressing a view (paragraphs 3.92 to 3.97).

Interim Damages

Need

6.37   We provisionally conclude that the practice of requiring those who seek an interim payment in personal injury cases to show a need for such a payment is supportable in principle. We would not wish to displace the court's discretion to grant an interim payment, unless that discretion is being exercised ungenerously. We seek comment on whether the latter is in fact the case (paragraph 4.4).

Effect of recoupment of DSS benefits

6.38   We note that interim awards granted for specific capital expenses can be absorbed or reduced by the new DSS recoupment regime. We suggest that such specific, or all, interim payments could be excluded from the regime, or the defendant could be required to make the interim payment cover the benefits paid out as well as the cost of the specific capital item required. We express no preference for a particular solution, but seek comment on how often the problem arises in practice, whether it actually discourages applications for interim awards, and whether and which of the proposed solutions would be effective (paragraph 4.5).

MIB as defendant

6.39   We note that case law establishes that where the Motor Insurers Bureau is a defendant in a personal injury action, the court has no jurisdiction to order the Bureau to make an interim payment. We provisionally conclude that this omission should be rectified (paragraph 4.6).

Procedural requirements

6.40   We note that the procedural requirements to seek an interim award create extra work for solicitors, and may deter applications. We note that it seems fair to the defendant that the plaintiff should justify the interim awards they seek. We ask whether consultees consider matters could be improved by solicitors increasing their efficiency or by simplifying the procedural requirements (paragraph 4.7).

Provisional Damages

Gradual deterioration

6.41   We provisionally conclude that the provisional damages regime should not be extended to include gradual deterioration in the plaintiff's condition (paragraph 5.6).

Recovery

6.42 We provisionally conclude that the provisional damages regime should not be extended to instances where the medical uncertainty concerns the extent to which the plaintiff will recover from an already existing condition (paragraph 5.8).

Time limits

6.43 We provisionally conclude that the flexibility of providing for time limits for applications for additional damages in R.S.C., O. 37, r. 8(2) should not be removed (paragraph 5.10).

Court's overriding discretion

6.44 We provisionally conclude that the court's overriding discretion to grant a provisional damages order should not be removed or narrowed (paragraph 5.11).

Only one application

6.45 We provisionally conclude that the court should be empowered, when approving the original provisional award, to allow for additional applications for further damages or to regard a second application arising from the same injury, though based on the same deterioration, as part of the same application. Alternatively, we suggest the court could have power in hearing the further application to permit specifically a further application again based on the same deterioration. We invite general comment on the need for such reform, and which solution is preferred (paragraph 5.12).

The Fatal Accidents Act 1976 and the Law Reform (Miscellaneous Provisions) Act 1934

6.46 We provisionally conclude that it would be desirable to legislate to remove the provisional damages regime from the ambit of section 1 of the Fatal Accidents Act 1976 (paragraph 5.20).

Structuring provisional awards

6.47 We provisionally conclude that it is desirable to facilitate the structuring of provisional, and indeed, interim, awards. We suggest this would require the recognition of court orders facilitating structured interim and provisional awards as a type of 'Model Agreement' qualifying for the favourable tax regime. It may also require amendment to the provisions of the provisional and interim regimes. We invite comment on this proposition (paragraph 5.21).

APPENDIX A

Table 1: Real and nominal interest rates and price inflation 1970-90

	Price Inflation %	Nominal Interest Rate %	Real Interest Rate %
1970	6.52	9.21	2.69
1971	9.18	8.85	-0.33
1972	7.48	8.90	1.42
1973	9.13	10.71	1.58
1974	15.94	14.77	-1.17
1975	24.05	14.39	-9.66
1976	16.62	14.43	-2.19
1977	15.91	12.73	-3.18
1978	8.20	12.47	4.27
1979	13.45	12.99	-0.46
1980	18.03	13.78	-4.25
1981	11.88	14.74	2.86
1982	8.70	12.88	4.18
1983	4.44	10.80	6.36
1984	5.01	10.69	5.68
1985	6.04	10.62	4.58
1986	3.40	9.87	6.47
1987	4.16	9.47	5.31
1988	4.92	9.36	4.44
1989	7.79	9.58	1.79
1990	9.44	11.08	1.64

Averages:

1970-90	10.01	11.54	1.52
1970-79	12.65	11.95	-0.70
1980-90	7.62	11.17	3.55

Notes:

1. Price Inflation is calculated as the rate of change of the Consumer Price Index.

2. The Nominal Interest Rate is based on the rate on 20 year British Government Securities.

3. Data taken from Economic Trends Annual Supplement, 1991.

Figure 1: Real interest rates 1970-90

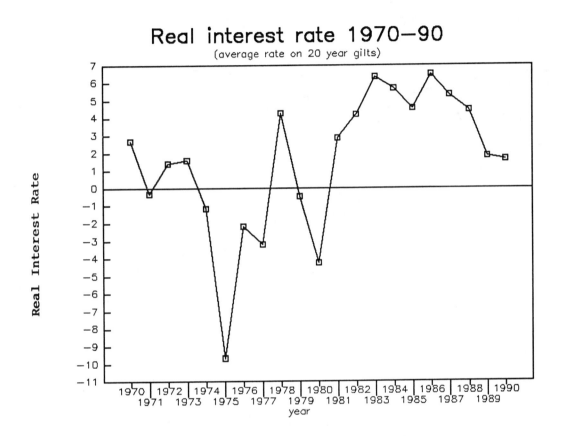

Note: Data taken from previous Table.

Figure 2: Interest rates and security yields 1990-92
(Reproduced from CSO Economic Trends, April 1992)

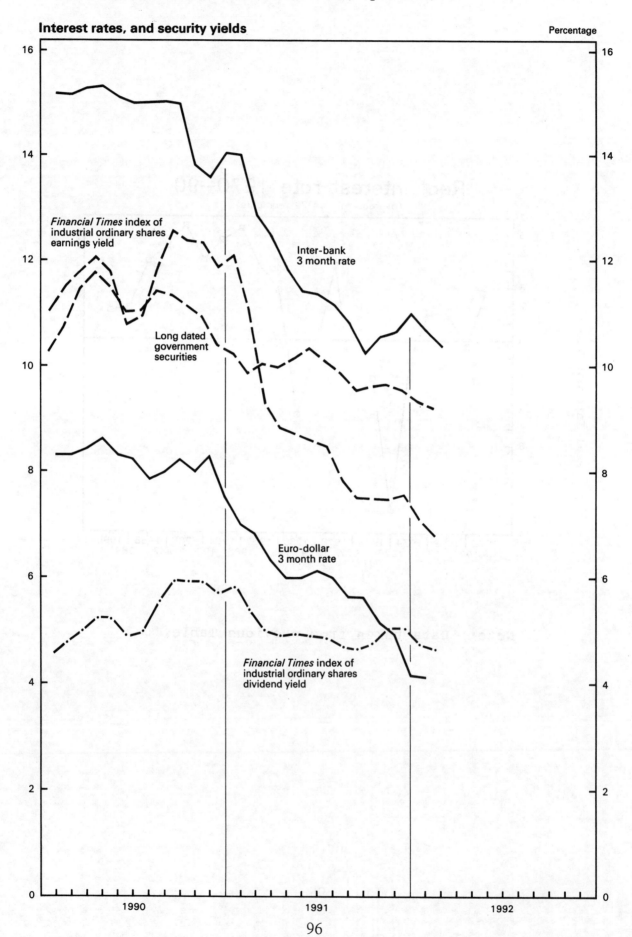

Interest rates, and security yields

Percentage

Financial Times index of industrial ordinary shares earnings yield

Inter-bank 3 month rate

Long dated government securities

Euro-dollar 3 month rate

Financial Times index of industrial ordinary shares dividend yield

1990   1991   1992

APPENDIX B

(i) The Ontario Courts of Justice Act, R.S.O. 1990, Chap. C.43, provides:

116.-(1) In a proceeding where damages are claimed for personal injuries or under Part V of the *Family Law Act* for loss resulting from the injury to or death of a person, the court,

(a)   if all affected parties consent, may order the defendant to pay all or part of the award for damages periodically on such terms as the court considers just; and

(b)   if the plaintiff requests that an amount be included in the award to compensate for income tax payable on the award, shall order the defendant to pay all or part of the award periodically on such terms as the court considers just.

(2) An order under clause (1)(b) shall not be made if the parties otherwise consent or if the court is of the opinion that the order would not be in the best interests of the plaintiff, having regard to all the circumstances of the case.

(3) In considering the best interests of the plaintiff, the court shall take into account,

(a)   whether the defendant has sufficient means to fund an adequate scheme of periodic payments;

(b)   whether the plaintiff has a plan or a method of payment that is better able to meet the interests of the plaintiff than periodic payments by the defendant; and

(c)   whether a scheme of periodic payments is practicable having regard to all the circumstances of the case.

(4) In an order made under this section, the court may, with the consent of all the affected parties, order that the award be subject to future review and revision in such circumstances and on such terms as the court considers just.

(5) If the court does not make an order for periodic payment under subsection (1), it shall make an award for damages that shall include an amount to offset liability for income tax on income from investment of the award. 1989, c.67, s.3.

****

(ii) The New South Wales Personal Injury Damages Bill 1991 provides specifically for structured settlements:

PART 4 - STRUCTURED SETTLEMENTS

Awards to which Part applies

18. This Part applies to an award of damages if:
(a) the plaintiff and the defendant have agreed that it is to apply; or
(b) the court considers that it should apply.

Court to determine arrangements for payment of damages

19. (1) In any award of damages to which this Part applies, the court is to order that any damages determined for future economic loss -+are to be paid in accordance with such arrangements as the court determines or approves.

(2) If the arrangements provide for the periodic payment of damages for deprivation or impairment of earning capacity, the arrangements must provide for those payments to be made at intervals of not more than 12 months.

Arrangements can provide for purchase of annuity

20. In making an order under this Part relating to damages for deprivation or impairment of earning capacity, the court may order that the damages be used to purchase an annuity for the plaintiff on such terms as the court thinks fit, but this section does not limit the court's powers under this Part.

Matters to be taken into account by court

21. In making an order under this Part, the court is to have regard to:

(a) the ability of the plaintiff to manage and invest any lump sum award of damages; and

(b) the views of any person who insures the defendant against the defendant's liability for the damages concerned; and

98

(c)   such other matter as the court thinks fit.

Variation or termination of arrangements

22.(1)A party to any arrangements determined or approved under this Part may apply to the court at any time for an order varying or terminating the arrangements.

(2) On an application under this section, the court may make such order as it thinks fit having regard to the provisions of this Part.

Regulations relating to structured settlements

23.   The regulations may make provision for or with respect to any matter dealt with in this Part and, in particular, may impose conditions or limitations on the orders that may be made under this Part or otherwise regulate the making of those orders.

****

APPENDIX C

Part II, Ord 29, r. 11 of the Rules of the Supreme Court -

11. - (1) If, on the hearing of an application under rule 10 in an action for damages, the Court is satisfied -

> (a) that the defendant against whom the order is sought (in this paragraph referred to as "the respondent") has admitted liability for the plaintiff's damages, or
>
> b) that the plaintiff has obtained judgment against the respondent for damages to be assessed; or
>
> (c) that, if the action proceeded to trial, the plaintiff would obtain judgment for substantial damages against the respondent or, where there are two or more defendants, against any of them,

the Court may, if it thinks fit and subject to paragraph (2), order the respondent to make an interim payment of such amounts as it thinks just, not exceeding a reasonable proportion of the damages which in the opinion of the Court are likely to be recovered by the plaintiff after taking into account any relevant contributory negligence and any set-off, crossclaim or counterclaim on which the respondent may be entitled to rely.

(2) No order shall be made under paragraph (1), in an action for personal injuries if it appears to the Court that the defendant is not a person falling within one of the following categories, namely -

> (a) a person who is insured in respect of the plaintiff's claim;
>
> (b) a public authority; or
>
> (c) a person whose means and resources are such as to enable him to make the interim payment.

[O.13, r. 12, of the County Court Rules (1991), Part 1, p. 241, incorporates the provisions of R.S.C. O.29, Part II, with minor modifications, so that the county court, in proceedings involving more than £500, can award interim payments.]

****

APPENDIX D

Section 32A of the Supreme Court Act 1981 as amended by
Section 6 of the Administration of Justice Act, 1982

ADMINISTRATION OF JUSTICE ACT 1982, S.6
Provisional damages for personal injuries

6.   Award of provisional damages for personal injuries

(1)   The following section shall be inserted after Section 32 of the Supreme
Court Act 1981 -

'32A.   Orders for provisional damages for personal injuries.

(1)   This section applies to an action for damages for personal
injuries in which there is proved or admitted to be a chance that at
some definite or indefinite time in the future the injured person
will, as a result of the act or omission which gave rise to the cause
of action, develop some serious disease or suffer some serious
deterioration in his physical or mental condition.

(2)   Subject to subsection (4) below, as regards any action for
damages to which this section applies in which a judgment is given
in the High Court, provision may be made by rules of court for
enabling the court, in such circumstances as may be prescribed, to
award the injured person -

> (a)   damages assessed on the assumption that the
> injured person will not develop the disease or suffer
> the deterioration in his condition; and

> (b)   further damages at a future date if he develops
> the disease or suffers the deterioration.

(3)   Any rules made by virtue of this section may include such
incidental, supplementary and consequential provisions as the rule-
making authority may consider necessary or expedient.

(4)   Nothing in this section shall be construed -

> (a)   as affecting the exercise of any power
> relating to costs, including any power to
> make rules of court relating to costs; or

(b)   as prejudicing any duty of the court under any enactment or rule of law to reduce or limit the total damages which would have been recoverable apart from any such duty.

(2)   In section 35 of that Act (supplementary) '32A', shall be inserted before '33' in subsection (5).

(3)   The section inserted as section 32A of the Supreme Court Act 1981 by subsection (1) above shall have effect in relation to county courts as it has effect in relation to the High Court, as if references in it to rules of court included references to county court rules.

[The relevant Rules of the Supreme Court are Order 37 rr. 7-10 (*Supreme Court Practice*, vol.1, pp.584-6). There is also an important Practice Direction (Practice Direction [1985] 1 W.L.R. 961). The regime also has effect in relation to County Courts (County Courts Act s 51; County Courts Rules O.6, r.1B; O.22, r.6.)]

****

Printed in the United Kingdom for HMSO
Dd294462 C18 11/92 G3397 10170

LIBRARY
DEPARTMENT OF SOCIAL SECURITY
ROOM 07/15 ADELPHI
1 - 11 JOHN ADAM STREET
LONDON   WC2N 6HT